BATTLE
OF THE
WILLS

All rights reserved. No part of this book may be reproduced, stored in a retrieval system, or transmitted in any form or by any means, electronic, mechanical, or otherwise, without the prior written permission of the publisher, except for brief quotations in articles and reviews.

Printed in the United States of America for Worldwide Distribution

Copyright © 2016 Elaine Mays

Print ISBN: 978-0-9759303-3-5
Ebook ISBN: 978-0-9759303-5-9

Verde Press

Cover design and interior design by Carol Webb of Bella Media Management

I dedicate this book to my son Alan who is always there for me.

Plant your own garden and decorate your own soul, instead of waiting for someone to bring you flowers.

~ Veronica A. Shoffstall

BATTLE
OF THE
WILLS

Elaine Mays

Introduction

This the story of my life. It has been a long and bumpy ride from the day I was born and I am sure many who read this will empathize with my experiences with a borderline dysfunctional family. I say borderline because we were, for all appearances the quintessential middle class, white family from small town America in the 1940's and 50's. We had a lovely home in the better part of town, went to church, and participated in community activities. My father was a business owner and worked with his brothers, contracting for homes and buildings in the community and provided an adequate living for this family of four. We vacationed every summer, often driving to Colorado and Montana to experience the beauty of that landscape.

My brother, who was six years older than me, was accomplished in his younger years, excelled in school, lettered in golf, took part in school plays and when I followed him six years later, the teachers always asked if I was Robert Boyer's sister. They all had a favorable opinion of him and I was expected to live up to that. Which I never could.

Underneath this disguise was something very dark; a brother who was terribly jealous and in fact hated his baby sister for being born and stealing his number one place in the family and who was diagnosed later in life with a mental illness and a mother who was likely mentally ill herself and unable to cope with the extreme sibling rivalry that ensued.

Growing up in a loveless family, I searched for love in other places and when I look back on my life I am amazed that I came through these times relatively unscathed. It could have gone the other way.

Even though, on many levels, this is a very sad story, it is also a story of how I survived and triumphed over adversity. I have reached a point in my life today where I have found my passion and purpose and I am living a life I never thought possible. While Robert died essentially a pauper and with few friends.

Many people have passed through my life over the years and I have written about them in this story. I have changed the names for some to protect their identity.

Chapter One

I got the call on a very hot Friday night late in July. I was in bed reading, preparing to go to sleep, the air conditioner cranking away, the ceiling fan whirring above, wearing a light cotton night gown with the sheets pushed back, trying to keep as cool as possible with the outdoor temperature still over 100 degrees. It was about 8 p.m. and I know that's early, but it's my usual time to go to bed; not much happens after that hour when you're seventy-six years old. The phone rang; I am one of a few people who still has a land line mainly because I use it for faxing and also because I find the quality of cell phone calls to be very bad and my hearing is not what it used to be.

Anyway, I answered with a simple "hello" and the woman calling said," Is this Elaine Mays?"

Now it's my behavior when I don't recognize a caller to ask "Who's calling?" so I know how to respond—either hang up on people trying to sell me something or continue to talk with them. But I didn't do that this time, for some reason.

I said, "Yes, this is Elaine Mays."

"This is Racheal (not her real name) calling from the San Bernardino Sherriff's office."

And I immediately thought, uh oh, something bad has happened.

"Are you Robert Boyer's sister?"

"Yes." Something bad has happened to him.

"I am calling to tell that your brother has passed away and his body is being held at Loma Linda Hospital where he died. Will you be taking care of his remains?"

I took a deep breath. Robert dead? I wasn't prepared for this. But then a person never is.

"I'm so sad," I said. "But I don't think I want to take care of his remains. I have been estranged from him after what he did to me thirteen years ago."

"There's a house," said Racheal.

"Oh, yes. The house." I hadn't thought about that.

"Here's my phone number. Give me a call if you change your mind."

"What happens to him if I don't take care of him?"

"You are the only relative?"

"Yes."

"He'll be buried in a pauper's cemetery."

I hung up the phone. And went back to bed. But I wouldn't sleep that night. All those memories came flooding back.

The next morning I called Racheal back. During the night I had thought long and hard about what I should do and decided, even though Robert treated me badly all of my life and especially after Mother died, he didn't deserve a pauper's burial. Earlier I had called the funeral home that had handled my mother's funeral in 1999, and also my grandmother's years before and asked them to give me quotes on how much it would cost to have Robert cremated. I told Racheal at the Sherriff's office I would to take care of Robert's remains and that the funeral home would be coming for his body that day.

BATTLE OF THE WILLS

They said they had been in contact with my brother's longtime friend and would I like to talk with him, and I said that would be fine.

Later that day, Biron called me back. I knew Biron from years back, and he had seemed like a good person. "I am so sorry to hear that Robert is gone." I offered my consolations. "This must be a sad time for you."

"Yes. It is. He had been ill for some time now. He'd had cancer a couple of years ago and had beat that, but about a year ago he got pneumonia, and his body was so weak from when he had cancer that he couldn't recover."

"Is there a will?" I had to ask.

"No. I couldn't find a will."

There's no will. Amazing, I thought. How could that be? Robert had been adamant that Mother have a trust to the point of being obsessed, so for him to not have a will was out of character.

"Is anyone living in the house?"

"No. There's no one there."

I called my financial advisor, whom I trust implicitly, to tell him the news about my brother. He said he was sorry for my loss and I thanked him. And then he asked when I was going to California.

"I guess I should go next week," I said with hesitation. The thought of driving over to Redlands was not pleasant. And then having to deal with my brother's death.

"You will need to secure the house, get his mail forwarded to you and you'll need a probate attorney. Let's see if we can find one for you in Redlands," he said. He pulled up the Martindale-Hubbell web site for me and we searched for a suitable probate attorney with a good rating.

I decided that I would make the drive the next week. I had to make arrangements before I could travel. I have two dogs and I called a pet sitter to come and stay in my home with them while I was gone. I travel often and normally I have my good friend, Ralph, who comes in to live with the dogs. They know him and adore him, and he feels the same for them, I think. But Ralph now has a full time job and that would mean that they would be outdoors all day long and with the heat, that would not be good. So I have a back-up. LuAnn lives in the next block, and she does pet sitting for a living. I know her and trust her to be in my home. And the dogs know her as well.

So I am good to go. I pack a few things and put some boxes in the back of my Honda Element thinking I will want to bring some things back with me. My mother had a set of Minton china, and if that's still there, I'll bring that back. Also the baby pictures and family photos if they're still there.

I take off on a Thursday morning at 8 a.m. hoping to be in Redlands four or five hours later. It's a straight shot on I-10 across the desert, through Quartzite, Blythe where the Colorado river runs down on to Mexico, then on up to the high desert, the Coachella Valley, elevation 1000 ft above sea level at the top, and then down to Indio, Palm Springs, Banning, Beaumont where there is a junction, highway 60 going to Riverside and I-10 continuing on to Calimesa, Yucaipa and then Redlands. It's an easy drive, if not somewhat tedious. I had made this drive many times when I visited Mother, years back. As I was driving across the desert I thought about the day we drove that route in 1973, when we were moving from Dublin, California to Phoenix. It was December and I had been living in Dublin with Alan our son, for four months until we could find a home and finally make the move. We were pulling a small U-Haul trailer as I recall with Warren's guns; he was a collector and he didn't trust the moving company. I am not a gun person. I really disliked the desert at that time, but I was willing to give it a try. And Warren had a good job and we had bought a beautiful home in an upscale neighborhood.

I have since changed my mind about the desert, and as I was driving, I noticed the subtle colors of limestone, iron ore and other minerals of the outcropping of rocks and small hills and mountains. The vegetation is thin, a few saguaros here and there, Joshua trees when I reached that area, soft green, lacy paloverde trees. There is a stark beauty found nowhere else in the world. I have grown to love the desert. And again, it took years. I had grown up in verdant (in the summer) Minnesota and lived in Northern California where it is green all year long. I remember thinking in those early days in Arizona how the forests of California were soft and sweet smelling and the desert was full of unfriendly, prickly plants. But the desert in bloom is a sight to behold.

So here I was driving across this desert to what had been the family home since 1982. My mother was gone and now my brother. I hadn't been back in sixteen years. What would I find when I got there? I had no idea.

As I drove down into the valley to Indio, I looked up at Mount San Jacinto looming large across the valley. Seeing it brought back memories of taking the tram to the top and one time when Alan joined me to camp overnight. It was one of the windiest nights I had ever spent in a tent. Then on to Banning, Beaumont, where the wind funnels down the valley, and they have now taken advantage of that wind with many turbines generating clean energy. It was quiet today. Then down again into another valley, and after what I thought was forever, the turnoff to Redlands.

I decided to visit the funeral home first to make sure they had retrieved Robert's remains. I had made the arrangements several days ago by telephone and over the internet. It took me awhile to find it; I hadn't been there in many years, but I finally did, parked and got out of the car. I walked up the steps of the vintage colonial building, opened the door and walked into the foyer. It was quiet and serene with blue carpet and blue Victorian drapes hanging on the windows, and the memory of my mother's funeral flooded my mind. It had been open casket—Robert made that decision—and the day before the funeral, I went to visit her a final time as she lay in her casket at the front of the small chapel. A nurse, a friend of Robert's was there as well, and I asked if she would leave for a while and give me some time alone with my mother. Then I went to the front and sat down and just looked at her and talked. She truly appeared as though she were sleeping and at peace. I told her that I always wanted to love her and wanted to be closer to her, but I didn't think she wanted that. It was too late now. I said goodbye and walked out. I know she had an unhappy life for the most part, much of her own making, although she had found some happiness in her later years, before her stroke.

Thinking about that day only made me want to make sure that the rest of my life would be free of strife as much as I could make it that way. And I was on my way to doing so. I thought about how I loved life, being happy and having fun. Then I went and talked to the funeral director, and he said that Robert's body had been retrieved and they would cremate him in a day or so. He said they would call me when it was done. I then paid and received two copies of his death certificate.

After leaving the funeral home, I went to visit my new attorney to meet him and get acquainted—see if I liked him. He was located in the largest building in downtown Redlands, the Citibank building on the 11th floor. I parked the car, went into the building and took the elevator up to his office. I hadn't made an appointment, but he was there, and his assistant said I could meet with him.

His name is Raymond (not his real name) but he prefers to be called Ray. I sat down in the chair on the other side of his executive desk. His office is large with windows overlooking the small downtown area of Redlands. Ray is young—in my terms given my age—he's good looking, dark hair, olive skin, looks to be physically fit and he's personable. We talk about the time leading up to the death of Robert. And about if there is no will, which appears to be true, then Robert has died in testate, without a will and his total estate goes to his nearest relative. Me. I am the only one left.

"Robert had a boyfriend," I tell Ray. "I am surprised he didn't leave his estate to him."

"Well he didn't. So you're it," Ray says. "You get everything."

At this point I wasn't sure what that meant. There is a house, but how many bills were there? And did he have any other assets? I didn't know.

Chapter Two

I leave his office and call Biron telling him to meet me at the house, which is only ten or fifteen minutes away. He has access and I need him to let me into the house. I intend to stay there for the next few days while I more or less take inventory of everything.

I do have a key, however, which I brought with me. But no way would this key open the door. It's been sixteen years since I had been to the house. The day my mother was buried. Surely Robert would have changed the locks in this amount of time.

And what would I find? Would my mother's things still be there? Would he have remodeled and changed everything? I did hear that his boyfriend, Jake (not his real name), moved in with him. I will soon know.

I drive up Citrus to Dearborn and turn into the complex. This home is an attached home, some call a condo, I call it a patio home. It has three bedrooms, the master suite has a walk-in closet (I would love to have a walk-in closet), two baths, living room with a fireplace—I've wanted to have a fireplace for years now—dining area, and an eat-in kitchen. It has a two car garage as well. There is quite a large patio out back where Robert planted roses and other flowers just for Mother. And it is an end unit, making it more desirable. The home is located on the eastern side of Redlands, where the oranges groves are still being tended. There is in fact an orange grove across the street from the house, which makes it seem like being in the country.

I remember the day I went to look at this home when Mother was deciding whether or not to buy it. She had been moving around from one apartment to another, and she needed a place like this that would be safe and a very pleasant place to live. She was unsure. They were asking over $90,000 for it, and she thought that was a lot of money; which it was in those days. But she had the cash: her inheritance from her father, my grandad.

I have to say that at that time, Robert had gone off to who-knows-where and Mother was alone. He didn't tell her where he was, didn't call her for about a year, and she was worried sick about him. I was living in Arizona, divorcing I think or something, living life I guess. I had come over to California especially to help her with this decision. I told her to buy it. She would never go wrong doing so. She would have a wonderful, safe place to live for a long time. The units were brand new. In fact, she would be the first one to buy there. And she did buy it.

I have to explain here also that basically my brother, Robert, never left my mother with the exception of a few short times in his life: when he was in the army, when my mother remarried, when she first moved to California after her second divorce. But he was with her for most of his life. He was gay and never married. Which I will tell you more about later.

She bought the condo and moved in, and it wasn't too long before Robert came back, out of money, a car full of dirty laundry, and she took him in. Of course.

So here I am all these years later about to step back into—I did not know what. I parked the car in front. Biron hadn't arrived yet. I walked up to the front door, put the key in the lock and turned it, and unbelievably, the door opened. I stepped inside. I was amazed. Not much had changed. There were a few pieces of furniture missing: my mother's writing desk, the coffee table. There was that yellow couch that I was never allowed to sit on (but the dog was), the yellow chair on the other side of the fireplace. Yellow was Mother's favorite color.

I walked back into the bedroom area. The master suite was much the same. But all of Mother's clothing was gone. Robert's room, no change except the carpet is very soiled from him being sick in there. The TV room, little change. The carpet very soiled in that room as well, but that had always been the case. They had allowed their little dog to wet in there, and I think Robert again being sick added to that. There was no odor though.

Biron walked into the house.

"Where's the writing desk?" I asked.

"Will has it."

I went over to greet him. I hadn't seen him in years. "Good to see you. Thanks for coming."

We walked into the kitchen. I looked out at the patio, and of course, after not being tended for months, the grass was overgrown, there were pine needles everywhere from the Aleppo pines that hovered overhead. The row of overgrown rose bushes along the back fence looked fairly healthy considering they had not been tended to in months. Needed a trim though.

We sat at the table, a—you guessed it—yellow wrought iron patio table with chairs to match in a kitchen with yellow floral wall paper.

"Were you with him when he died?"

"No. But I had visited that day."

"So tell me what happened."

Biron told me again how Robert had esophageal cancer a couple of years ago and he came through it. But that he was weakened from the chemo and about a year ago he became ill again this time with pneumonia and his body couldn't fight it.

"Well, given his age, it's not surprising. He was six years older than me, you know. That would make him 82."

"I thought you were quite a bit younger."

"Six years. So when I was born, he'd been the top dog in the household for six years and I stole his thunder. He was always competing with me. If we had been baby birds, he would have pushed me out of the nest early. And he tried. He hated me from day one. Tried to smother me with a pillow, locked me in a closet for hours several times."

"He told everybody what an evil person you were. Said you killed your mom."

"I know. Robert wasn't well you know."

There was a silence. Biron said he had things to do, but that we should have dinner tomorrow night. That sounded good to me. I would be exhausted no doubt from going through the family photos if they were still there and other stuff in the house. I wasn't going to clean it out altogether yet, until we filed for probate. Then likely I would have to come back, get everything out, and prepare the house for sale.

As Biron left the house he turned to me and asked, "But where was Jake?"

I shook my head not knowing how to answer. Jake was Roberts's lover for several years. In fact, he had lived with Robert in this house.

Chapter Three

I spent the afternoon looking through some photos and books in some boxes. Someone had gone through things, probably Biron, and put some of the knickknacks, china and glassware on the dining room table. I noticed that the original oils were still on the walls; I would take those back with me. But when I looked for Mother's china, I couldn't find it. And as I went through the house it seemed like the place had been frozen in time. He still had two old analogue TV's that he converted with cable. The appliances had not been upgraded. The light fixtures were the same and the lamps had the old incandescent light bulbs. It was like the house was frozen in time from sixteen years ago.

There were some boxes of books and photos on the dining room floor and as I started to sort through the family photos, I went back in time to a childhood that was on the one hand ideal and on the other filled with despair and sorrow. We grew up in a picturesque small town in Minnesota. We had a lovely home in the best part of town that my father had built for us. My father was a contractor and had a gravel pit north of town that supplied sand and gravel for many of the buildings and homes in the area and he worked together with his brother, Henry, who built silos for the local farmers.

Our house wasn't opulent by today's standards, but it was more than adequate; built of cement block with three roomy bedrooms, only one bathroom, upstairs, living room with a bay window and a fireplace, dining room and a large eat in kitchen. I say large because as I grew older, Robert and I were many times responsible for cleaning and waxing the linoleum kitchen floor, and it was a big job. There were two open porches, one off the kitchen and another over the two car garage. And there was a basement where the furnace was and where my mother did the laundry. The house sat on a huge lot with a maple and a spruce tree in front and an elm tree, a birch tree and a crab apple tree in the back yard. We had a garden every summer that was always a family project. In the early days, a man would come to plow with a horse but in later years he had a tractor and I used to sit on the fender while he plowed. We planted corn, beans, tomatoes, potatoes and we had a raspberry patch.

We always had pets galore; a red cocker spaniel named Ginger, and when he died, another cocker spaniel, Buffy. We also had a cat. We called her Mama Kitty because she had so many kittens. I recall one time when she was having her kittens and I wanted to watch, but Mother wouldn't allow it. That could have been a teaching moment, but sex was verboten in our household. We finally took Mama Kitty to a friend's farm where they needed cats to keep the mice population in control, and we kept one of her kittens, a black and white male that we named Tucky. I guess my parents thought that if they had male cats and dogs they wouldn't have to deal with reproduction. Which is true they didn't, but our male animals were out there breeding, like it or not. Spaying and neutering in their minds was "unnatural". I think most people of that time thought that way. But then our male dogs were often running off—we had

BATTLE OF THE WILLS

no fences, and we'd get a call from a neighbor that our dog was hanging around their house trying to mate with their female dog.

Periodically we also had ducks, a chicken, snakes, rabbits, and turtles. And one time, my father brought home two sheep. His great idea was that they could eat the grass, we had a huge lawn, and he wouldn't have to mow it. This was before Robert took over that job. We were the hit of the neighborhood. All of the kids from blocks away came to play with and ride the sheep. Dad eventually decided they were too much trouble; sure they ate the grass, but unevenly and they dropped many sheep dung around the yard, so he took them back to the farm.

When we went on vacation every summer, we had to find people to take care of our menagerie. Some of the animals went back to the farm, like the chicken and the ducks, while the dog went to the kennel and a neighbor often took care of the cat. The year that we had the ducks, when we got home that summer, I asked where my pet ducks were and Dad said they stayed on the farm. I know Mother hated the ducks because they pooped all over the back porch, so I thought that she was responsible for that decision. I cried though; I loved those ducks as I loved all of the animals that we had.

As I looked through the photos, I saw the ones taken on our family vacations in the summer: in the Black Hills where we visited Mt. Rushmore, on McDonald Lake in Glacier National Park and standing in front of the geysers at Yellowstone National Park. And for several years we stayed on a guest ranch in Rocky Mountain National Park where I had my own horse every summer. I loved horses not unlike many girls my age.

I thought about how underneath the façade of a happy family of four, there was something not quite right. And over the years it would take shape in an ugly way.

I went to bed that night feeling very strange about my

surroundings, like there were ghosts lurking about the near empty house, although I am not a believer in such things. I was uncomfortable being alone in this house with so many memories. I finally went to sleep.

Chapter Four

I worked most of the next day wrapping up the china and knickknacks sitting on the dining room table. There were two Hummel figurines, a boy with a scarf, standing and a girl holding a flower. Where was the third, a girl sitting holding a bird? Some pieces of china, vases. Much of this I would take back and donate. I couldn't keep it. My house was full as it was.

Biron showed up about five p.m., and he drove us to a nearby family restaurant. I bought dinner, and we talked about family and friends of Robert.

I asked if his other friends had stuck by my brother, and he said no they were mostly gone.

"What about Jake?" I asked.

"Yes, what about Jake. Where was he? Why didn't he show up?" Biron implored.

I had briefly met Jake many years ago, right before Mother died. Robert was visiting me in Phoenix, a rare occasion, and Jake, a truck driver, was meeting him here. We met at the drugstore near my home. I recall that he was a large man with a gut, almost black curly hair, and I think he had a beard and a mustache. Much younger than Robert. Very personable and articulate, though.

"Jake should have been here," Biron said.

I asked Biron when Jake was last here with Robert. And Biron told me that he left Robert as soon as he found out that Robert was sick with cancer.

We talked some more about family, and then bought some desert to take back to the house to eat.

When were back sitting at the kitchen table Alan, my son, called, trying to give moral support, and we talked for a while. Biron dialed a number on his cell phone and talked for few minutes and then he said, "Jake's on the line. Do you want to talk to him?"

"Sure."

Biron handed me the phone. "Hello, Jake. Long time no talk. How are you?"

Jake said he was fine and then he said, "I have a will. Signed and notarized."

"You do? An original will?"

"Yes."

And I just said okay and then said goodbye to him. Well, I guess that does that. I wasn't surprised. Given this development, I might as well pack up and go home. If Jake has a valid will, then that means that I will not inherit anything. But first I wanted to see the will. Jake said that Robert's attorney, Gary, (not his real name) had drawn up the will. This was the same attorney that did the trust for Mother. I needed to meet with him and see if I could get a copy of the will. And the next day I did. When I went to his office he complained about how when Robert was last in his office several years ago, he kept talking about how I killed Mother. Gary told Robert that that was a bunch of bunk.

I brought a copy of the draft of the will to the house and read it. Basically it left everything to Jake, except a large chunk of money to Biron and some to Will, another friend. I didn't think that money even existed. So if in fact Jake did have the original, signed and notarized will, he would get the house and of course I would get nothing. Now I was okay with that to a point. If that's what Robert had wanted. After being estranged from Robert for so many years, I expected nothing from his estate. This whole turn of events was something I didn't think would ever happen. And I didn't need the money. I had planned well for my retirement, worked hard in the computer industry for twelve years or more making a decent amount of money, maxed out my 401K, saved the rest, and I had inherited some from Mother when she died even though Robert tried to get it all. I am not a greedy person.

The next day Biron came over with a hand written will leaving most everything to Biron and nothing to Jake. One problem though, it wasn't Robert's handwriting and it wasn't his signature either. When I showed this will to my attorney, he said it was a holographic will and to be valid, if it wasn't Robert's handwriting, there should be a statement saying that in the document. He said this will would not hold up.

Then Biron said he thought there was yet another will that Robert had written after Jake left him. And for the next couple of days, I searched the house for that will or any others that might exist. There were files of documents, bunches of them, mostly lawsuits. And reams of paper copies of documents from the law suit when Mother died in 1999. Since Robert had sued me in 2000 for allegedly killing my mother, he had brought several law suits against various people, an apartment complex, the HOA. I was an add-on to the suit when Mother died; he was mainly suing the doctor, the nursing home and the hospital. My attorney at that time, Ramon, in California called me after it was settled and said that Robert had been awarded $600,000. Now had he actually collected that money, I doubt it. I think the other litigants likely appealed and either reduced the amount or wiped it out entirely. Robert often told people he had a million dollars. But that was a lie. He was actually broke at the time of his death. I had found $400,000 in one money market fund back in 2004, but that was gone. And without even tracking the funds, it was obvious that he had just pissed the money away. Biron told me that Robert bought two vehicles for Jake, a truck and a car. That's at least 60 K right there. And I found canceled checks written to Jake, paying him money every week for months, maybe years, in the amounts of anywhere from $100 to a $1000. Was Robert buying Jake, trying to make him stay? Very likely. So sad. Robert must have been desperate.

I called a couple of his other attorneys and they said they hadn't done a will for my brother. One of them wouldn't even talk to me, and when I pressed the issue, his assistant said he was not doing any work for my brother. I told her that Robert was dead; she said nothing.

By the end of the week I was ready to go home. I had searched the house thoroughly and found no other will. I was also looking for tax returns to get a handle on how much money in cash or savings he really had. There were none.

Likely if what Jake said was true, the estate would go to him. All I could do at this point was try to get all of the family photos and letters out of the home and leave. The furniture and everything else would be left there for Jake to do what he wanted.

I packed the day before I was to leave, and the Element was stuffed, four original paintings, a huge box full of dishes and mementos, boxes of photos, letters and documents, my grandmother's lamp—I couldn't get anything else in the car. And I possibly would never return to this house. There were two little maple occasional chairs that I couldn't get into the car and I didn't want Jake to have them. I think Mother bought them back in the 30's soon after Robert was born. I had seen them in photos of that time. I grew up with them, spending many hours reading in those chairs as a child, and then they were in my home for a while when I was newly married, but I returned them to Mother sometime in the 80's I think. I couldn't leave them behind, so I asked a neighbor if she would keep them until I could make arrangements to have them shipped, and she was agreeable to that.

The next morning I was preparing to leave. I went to the neighbor's to thank her for her help, and we had coffee and talked. I told her all about my crazy life, maybe too much, but thought she was a friend. Found out later that she wasn't.

Biron came by with Robert's car that he had been keeping at his house. It was a 2000 Ford Torino with over 200 thousand miles on it, not worth a lot. If Robert had been a millionaire, I would think he would have had a newer car. The car did have leather seats however.

I had to take Biron back to his house in San Bernardino before I could leave. As we were driving, Biron said, "You're not at all like what Robert said you were."

"And what did he say I was like?" As if I didn't know.

"He said you were really mean and nasty. But you're very nice and easy to get along with."

"Robert hated me. For whatever reason. I think he was just not well. I wanted us to be friends, but it wasn't to be."

Chapter Five

I was on the way to Indio by ten o'clock, much later than I had intended. It was a bright sunny day with some high clouds. I would get into Phoenix by maybe three or so. I missed my dogs. I was glad to be going home.

As I was driving up the grade coming out of the valley from Palm Springs and Indio, I thought of the many times I had made this drive in the past and recalled how every time I was leaving, I felt the relief to be driving away from my family, my mother and Robert. Every visit was painful. Robert was always acting out, throwing tantrums, and Mother was depressed. I recall how on one visit, Robert was screaming at my mother about how no one was helping him and everyone he knew had help. There was no talking to him, but I thought about how all of his life he had had support and he was being helped right then and there; he paid no rent to my mother for living in her home and he had food to eat. I know she paid for his toupees. He had become bald early in life. Then I thought about how I was the one who had no help, but I didn't want it. I had to be independent.

The last two times were especially emotional. I had visited

Mother in the hospital, and she was very ill and confined to her bed. She didn't recognize me, couldn't eat and I had said to the doctor and Robert that maybe it was time to let her go. So when I was leaving that next day, he screamed at me "You want to kill your Mother!" I cried all the way back to Phoenix. I realized later he was setting me up for the law suit, but I didn't know it then. And the last time was the day after the funeral. Robert and I were talking to a neighbor, who was a doctor in fact, and he mentioned that he was going to sue, and of course we didn't believe him. Why would anyone sue for wrongful death for a person who was eighty-eight years old, who had a stroke and was never going to recover?

    For the rest of the drive all the memories came back. And part of me thought that maybe I should have been there for Robert when he was ill. But for thirteen years after separating myself from him, I'd had a more or less peaceful life, with the exception of the two years of fighting breast cancer in 1970. And there was nothing I could have done for him, and I could just imagine him saying to me that all I wanted was the inheritance. The last time I talked with him was when the law suit ended. He had settled with me, and I had prevailed in getting my half of my mother's estate which was all I wanted. I called him on the phone. I hadn't talked with him at all when the law suit was going on. But now I wanted some family photos and my baby pictures, which I knew he had. He said to me that *he* would make copies of them, and then I could pay him. I hung up. I never talked with him again. I knew he was all about making trouble for me. But knowing that he was "not well", should I be taking care of him? No. My life was worth something, and I was determined that the rest of my life would be happy. And he was going to be okay. He had shelter, the house, and he had money. He also had this boyfriend. I would walk away and not worry. And that was what I did. But I always thought about the photos; would

BATTLE OF THE WILLS

I never see them again? So I pictured a fire; the photos were lost in a fire and there was nothing I could do. They were gone.

I spent the next week going through the things that I had brought back with me, the letters and photos from my childhood, some from way before when Mother was a child. Those memories I had put away for the past thirteen years came back. The last ten years before Mother died were some of the worst. But again I had tried to distance myself from them and only visited a couple of times a year. Looking through the cards and letters, I did write to Mother often and I sent Christmas cards and Mother's day cards, Valentine's Day cards, Easter cards. They were always sent with love in my heart. But those last few years, when I sent Christmas presents, they would send them back. So I stopped sending gifts and sent flowers instead. As I look back now, I realize a couple of things, my mother was under siege from Robert, and I think she didn't know what to do. And I couldn't help. If I said anything to her that was in least bit negative about him, she lashed out at me. She was protecting him. And yet, I think Robert was telling Mother terrible lies about me. But I will tell you more about that later.

Throughout the week, the more I thought about Mother's house, even though it was Robert's house now only because he'd inherited it from Mother, the more incensed I became that this man, this stranger to our family, was going to inherit it and make a lot of money from its sale. Mother paid for that house with money that she inherited from her father, my grandfather who had worked many years to save that money. It was just wrong. I called my financial advisor and talked with him, telling him how I felt, and he advised me to speak with an attorney about contesting the will. And so I did that; I called an attorney in Arizona and he said that I should talk to someone in California due to laws differing from one state to another. I did have my attorney, but he had already told me I would probably not win because Robert would have had to be totally out of it at the time of the signing of the will. So I called another attorney and told him the circumstances of Robert's mental illness. He had been diagnosed with paranoid schizophrenia in the early 70's, and I felt Jake had taken advantage of him. He gave me the same advice.

I decided to write a letter to Gary with a copy to Ray, my probate attorney, telling him my concerns about my brother's mental illness, that he had not been able to hold a job in years and had been more or less taken care of by Mother, and that when Mother died, he'd suffered the loss of her death and turned to Jake, and that Jake took advantage of Robert. I also said that Mother used the inheritance from Grandpa, who'd worked all of his life, to buy the home. And I have a son who should inherit from this estate. I told him that Jake was with Robert only a few years, and when Robert became ill, he left and never returned.

I sent the letter off knowing it likely would not help, but it made me feel better just venting and letting them know how this had played out. I thought if Jake had been a long time partner or if they had been married and Jake had been there for Robert when he was sick, I would be okay with having him inherit the estate. But it wasn't like that. Apparently Jake left Robert when he needed him most.

I kept going through the papers and photos. I found a certificate written to Grandpa in 1907, saying that he, Ernest Wakefield Franklin, had finished apprenticeship as a machinist with the Mankato Machine Company in Mankato Minnesota and was highly recommended. I searched the company on the internet and discovered they are still in existence today.

My grandfather, one of eight children, as he told us when he was living, was born on a farm in Quebec Canada,. He left home when his mother, Hannah, died when he was thirteen years old. He traveled across Canada working the wheat fields, eventually ending up in Winnipeg Canada. He then traveled south to Mankato where I think he had a cousin. And that was where he met my grandmother, Leone. Grandma had graduated from State Normal and was a school teacher in a one room school. She told me stories about how difficult it was for her to come to school every day where she had to chop and bring in the firewood in the winter—winters are cold in Minnesota—besides start the fire in the stove to warm the school. She was a tiny woman, maybe 4 ft 10 inches tall.

They married and moved to St Paul where Grandpa took a job with Waterman-Waterbury, a company in Minneapolis that manufactured oil furnaces where he worked for many years. The company is no longer in existence. And Grandma worked for a short time for the newspaper as a proof reader. But then Grandpa built a little bungalow on Drew Avenue in Minneapolis. When I say built, he did most of the work himself.

Grandma became pregnant with my mother, and she was born on January 25th, 1911. I think that being such a small woman, Grandma had a difficult birth, and she decided never to have another child. Mother, of course was born at home with the doctor attending. And so Grandma being Catholic, abstinence was the only form of birth control for her. Now I don't know the full story, but as long as I knew my grandparents, they had separate bedrooms. I think Grandma might have avoided sex as much as she could, maybe they never had sex after my mother was born, I don't know. Which was not good for the marriage. But they stayed together for sixty some years, partners in many ways, but living a contentious life. When Grandma died, she was eighty-eight years old, and Grandpa said that he was happier than he had ever been.

After my mother was born, they decided they needed a larger home and so my grandfather built a second larger home on Abbott

Avenue, near Lake Harriet, and this was the home that I visited many times as a child. It was a two story, with two porches on the back and a large porch on the front on a small corner city lot. He built this home while still holding down a full time job. I actually saw the house in 1998 when I went back to Minnesota for my fiftieth high school reunion and talked to the woman who owned it. I even talked her into letting me come inside, which my son, who was with me said was rude, but I wanted to see it. And I communicated with this woman for a couple of years after.

I idolized my grandfather. He was a self-made man with only an eighth grade education and yet he worked hard all of his life, and because they were savers, even though he never made a lot of money, they had a sizable nest egg when he retired. But they always had a fine home, the best and latest appliances, a new car. Grandma loved to sew, and she made most of her clothes, and I learned that from her.

Grandpa was very health conscious, jogged to keep fit way before anyone else was doing this and taught me how to run the distance when I was maybe twelve years old. We would jog together around Lake Harriet when I was visiting. He was also aware of eating good nutritious food; he loved bran muffins and oatmeal. He was my role model.

In later years he was hired by the University of Minnesota, and because he was so good at what he did, they awarded him an honorary engineering degree. He lived to be ninety-five years old. Robert told me before Mother died that Grandpa was part Native American, and I could see that in his facial features and how he had very little facial hair.

Another week went by and I decided that I needed to have a copy of this will that Jake said he had. So I called Gary and asked him to send me a copy. His assistant, Shelley (not her real name), told me that they didn't have it yet. Jake was in process of getting it to them. He had Fedexed it, and it should be there by the weekend.

"Would you send me a copy when you receive it?" I asked.

Shelley assured me that I would receive a copy.

I asked if they had received my letter, and she said they had.

Chapter Six

I was three years old when I ran away from home the first time. I remember it to this day. In the summer Mother would often put me in a playpen in the back yard thinking I would be contained and she could go about her housework without having to chase me around. Sometimes I had a companion, our family dog, a red cocker spaniel named Ginger. By this time Ginger was getting up there in years, but he still put up with my "abuse" of pulling his ears and poking his eyes. He was a good dog.

I hated being confined, didn't like being in the baby buggy, couldn't see where we were going—yes I remember that. I hated being in the high chair for any length of time—I remember that too.

I had been working on getting out of the playpen for some time. It was a wooden playpen with slates strategically placed, making it difficult to climb up and over. But I kept at it and this one day I was successful. Now I also remember what I felt once I was free; I didn't quite know what to do. But I took off with my fat little legs and went down the street and up another and ended up maybe two blocks over before my big brother found me. And I was crying.

I think this was the metaphor for my life. Escape. I have, up until the last few years, been wanting to get away, and then when I get there, I never know what to do with myself. Fortunately, I am beyond that now.

Robert was six years old when I was born—we were both born in May. It had to have been a shock for him as up until then he had been the kingpin, the only child, receiving all the adulations from family and friends. And along came me; I was chubby and cute—a Gerber baby, and people fawned over me. Mother called me honey pink and kept saying to everyone how much Robert wanted a baby sister, but I don't think she was convincing, especially for him. As I grew and we would be playing in the house, he would put a pillow over my face and try to smother me until I could hardly breathe. He often put me in a store room, locked the door and left me in the dark for hours. Other times he would get me down on the floor and spit on my face. He clearly wasn't happy having a little sister. And yet I tried to look up to him as my big brother. When I tell people about this, which is very seldom, they ask how he got by with these antics, but Mother was often gone for hours at a time. I don't know where—shopping, visiting friends—and she left my brother, who was maybe ten or so at the time, to be in charge. We seldom had babysitters; my parents hardly ever went out in the evening.

After I was born, I think Mother was having second thoughts about having a second child. She often told me about how, since I was such a large baby, over eight pounds, I had torn up her insides and she had to have major surgery. I remember when she had the surgery and how painful it was for her. And then she told me once that her mother told her not have a second child. That one was enough.

As I grew up, I was always getting into trouble, jumping in mud puddles, climbing trees, playing in the dirt. I never wanted to come home after a day of play, and Mother had to search the

BATTLE OF THE WILLS

neighborhood for me and call me in for dinner at night. Because we lived in an almost a rural setting, we had free reign to roam the neighborhood wherever we pleased, play our games and come home for mealtime. That doesn't exist today. I had a couple of friends in the next block. One of them, Jeanie, was my best friend and we did sleepovers and played "horse"—yes we pretended to be horses on our hands and knees. I constantly had callouses on my knees in those days—I think up until I was maybe eight or so. And if people think young children are not sexually aware, they would be wrong. We were conscious of our sexuality; when playing "horse" we pretended to breed and have "foals". We explored each other's bodies when we had sleepovers. I remember we would hide under Jeanie's brother's bed trying to see him naked. He found us and was really angry.

And then another time I recall, there was a little boy about our age in the neighborhood and he asked us, Jeanie and me, if we wanted to see his we-we. Jeanie hesitated, but then I said yes, and he took down his pants and showed us. Mother found out about it and I got a whipping; I recall sitting under the dining room table crying my eyes out.

I was often the bad child and Robert was the good one. He worked around the house, mowed the lawn and helped paint the house. And I tried as much as I could to get out of doing any household chores. I was often being punished and to redeem myself I would diligently dig in and clean up the kitchen and wash the dishes, so I was doing my share in a roundabout way. I tried to put that aside. I just wanted to have fun. And to this day that is what my life is all about; having fun.

Even though, it was in many ways the ideal childhood. We played hard, winter and summer. In the winter we built snow forts and had snow ball fights with teams from neighbor children on the block. And because we had all of that open space with a golf course across the street, it was our winter playground, for sledding, snow shoeing. Playing Yukon King was one of my favorites, pretending to be an officer in the far north enforcing the law. In the summer we played cops and robbers, cowboy, and sometimes movie stars. Then we'd go into Jeanie's attic and put on her mother's clothes: long fancy gowns, a feather boa, and wonderful hats. They were much more glamorous than my mother's clothing. We made up stories and played out scenarios of love stories like soap operas. We entertained ourselves.

Then at night with the long summer evenings, all the kids in the neighborhood would gather and we'd play kick the can, hide and seek, blind man's bluff and other games until dark, which in the north is near ten o'clock.

In my teen years, Jeanie and I grew apart and found other friends. Sadly her father, Gordon, died of cancer. He was a smoker. And her mother, Betty, would never recover from the loss. Jeanie moved out of the house in her senior year in high school, because she and her mother were not getting along. When Jeanie came back one day to check on her mother, she found her in the car in the garage. She had asphyxiated herself.

From the time I was six months old, until 1945, America was at war after the bombing of Pearl Harbor December 7, 1941. I recall seeing my favorite Uncle Harlan off at the train station to serve in the army when I was three years old. Fortunately he came home unharmed. But the war years as I remember them were lean years for most everyone. We had rationing of sugar and other staples including gasoline. Mother could not buy silk stockings as Japan produced the silk and silk was used for parachutes and tires. And we couldn't buy automobiles; the factories were dedicated to making airplanes and guns and other war materials. In 1941 we were just coming out of the great depression of the 30's. But we were fortunate, our family had plenty. My father bartered with businesses in the area for food and other things.

For several years we went to grandmother's home in Faribault, my father's mother, every Sunday for dinner, and war and politics were the topics of the day. Then I went home at night and dreamt about airplanes bombing our little house. The dream was about me playing in the living room and the bombers were coming across the golf course and they could see me through bay window. I remember how I would wake up in a sweat. It was a glorious day when the war ended in May of 1945. I recall riding my tricycle up and down the sidewalk that day waving a small American flag.

It was during those years that I was a bed wetter, I would say until I was maybe four or five. I would wake up in the early morning hours, the bed soaked, and I would lay there until morning, cold and wet and not knowing what to do. I grew out of it eventually. Fortunately, I was never punished, but I can picture my brother helping my mother carry my mattress out of the house to dry and the look of rebuke on Robert's face.

Mother then thought that I had a urinary problem, and we spent the next five years with doctors trying to cure my malady. I did often have what is now called UTI, urinary tract infection. I was taken to the University Hospital in St. Paul and to the Mayo Clinic in Rochester. The good part was that we took the train, an old steam train, and it was an adventure. But I spent much time, especially in the winter, in bed. I had to wear snow pants to school, which I hated. And they tried several different medications and antibiotics, which were expensive for the time. There was no health insurance in those days. Eventually I grew out of that as well. But when I look back, it was pretty simple. My anatomy was partly the cause and keeping that area clean when I went to the bathroom. There are natural cures now: drinking an acidic juice like grapefruit juice and flushing out the bladder with lots of water.

Mother and the doctors were fearful that if the infection migrated to my kidneys, potentially it could have been fatal. In fact, I had a dear friend in college, my roommate in my freshman year, who died from kidney disease.

The holidays were a special time in our household. We usually went to Grandma's house in Minneapolis for Thanksgiving. It was often a snowy trip in our brown 1937 Plymouth with a small space heater and running boards. We had that car until 1942 when the automobile factories were making cars again after the war. It seemed that every year we would receive the largest snowfall the week before Thanksgiving. To drive away from our home, we had to drive out the long driveway in the back, to the alley and then to the street. I can remember one time when there were huge drifts in the driveway and the alley, and so my father, who was always a problem solver, drove around the side of the house and across the front yard.

The tempo increased as Christmas approached. In the early days of my life we visited the farm to buy our fresh turkey. I loved seeing all of the animals, the cows in the warm barn and the pigs with little piglets. We would buy fresh eggs from the farm as well. We spent hours picking out the best tree from the nursery, and I was freezing by the time we made up our minds. And then I would sit and wait for Santa. As I grew a little older and had figured out that Mom and Dad were Santa, I would search the house to try and find the gifts I had asked for. Shame on me. As a teenager, I was expected to help with the Christmas dinner. Mother and I would be up at midnight making the last minute preparations. Everything was made from scratch; cranberry sauce, pumpkin pies, turkey stuffing.

I have fond memories of that time of year. I loved seeing the manger scenes placed around town and one at the public library every year. That would not be allowed today. Our living room was filled with the scent of pine from the fresh cut spruce tree, decorated with glass ornaments, tinsel and colored lights. On Christmas Eve we went to church and when we came home we always had a fire burning brightly in the fireplace. We hung our stockings for Santa and had hot cocoa and Christmas cookies. Then it was off to bed where I slept very little in anticipation of seeing the presents under the tree in the morning.

Sometimes I would walk outdoors in the fresh snow and marvel at the Christmas lights in all of the houses. I'd catch snowflakes in my mittens, so intricate, each one unique. At night the snow sparkled; I called it diamonds in the snow. It was truly a magical time of year, albeit very cold. But when you are young you don't notice. Come January, however, the cold and the snow became old very fast. We often had thirty degrees below zero, and the snow sometimes lasted until late March; those were long dark winters. When I became an adult and after I married, I didn't appreciate the snow in the least. It had to be shoveled and driving on icy, snowy roads was a pain. That was one reason why my husband and I decided to move to California and as I look back that was one of the best decisions of my life. Although I went back to Minnesota for my fiftieth high school reunion in July of 1998 and it was beautiful. But July in Minnesota often is.

One Christmas when my mother was preparing the dinner, I looked in the sink and saw what looked like two chickens thawing in the sink. I asked my mother what they were, and she told me they were ducks. Well, I put two and two together and figured those were my pet ducks. When I asked her she wouldn't say. I was crushed. Needless to say I didn't eat any meat that Christmas day for dinner.

I said earlier that we often went to my maternal grandmother's for

Thanksgiving and then had Christmas at home and my mother's parent's sometimes joined us. I can't remember a time when we spent a holiday with my father's mother. She was a widow and lived alone. As time went on and when I look back now remembering conversations between my parents, I don't think she liked my father's family at all. Even though they lived in our town, we spent very little time with them. We did visit his sister Doris and her husband Walter in New Ulm occasionally. I think they were wealthy, lived in a big house on a bluff overlooking the town. He owned and operated the newspaper and the TV station in the area, and when I looked him up on the internet—Walter Mickelson was his name—he was considered an early media mogul.

My father's other sister, Wilma, was a school teacher in Milwaukie Wisconsin, and in fact taught in what would be considered a ghetto area of the city made up of mostly blacks and minorities and during the summer months traveled the world. She never married that I knew of, but when I looked up her obituary on the internet, she did have a different last name, so she may have married after our family split which would have been about 1953. She was my favorite aunt and I called her my Aunt Willie. When I was three or so she gave me a rag doll, like Raggedy Ann, only black, and I still have that doll to this day, although it is in bad shape from being "mauled" by one of my dogs. She gave me my first novel to read when I was twelve, the Hound of the Baskervilles. Of course there was a great rift in the family when my mother divorced my father, but I'll tell you more about that later.

I hadn't heard from Gary and was wondering if he had received the will from Jake. I called over there and talked with Shelley, and she said that Jake would be sending the will that weekend.

The more I thought about Jake inheriting a house that my mother bought with my grandfather's money, the angrier I became.

This couldn't happen. But there was probably little I could do about it. If the will that Jake had was valid, it would all go to him. Very sad. I know one thing though, Robert would never have wanted me to have any of it, and I hadn't even thought about inheriting anything from him. I thought he might even have gotten married. I hadn't talked with him in thirteen years.

It wasn't like I needed the money. I am financially secure. I worked very hard as an IT professional for twelve years. I maxed out my 401K and was very frugal in my spending habits; just like my grandparents. When I divorced the first time, I was awarded a lump sum of money, albeit not enough for the seventeen years of marriage. I put half of that money down on a house and the rest in the bank for emergency. I still live in that little house today.

Chapter Seven

We weren't a religious family. Although as I was sorting through the old papers from our childhood, I saw that Robert belonged to several church youth groups as did I when I was in high school. We were both baptized in the church, and I went to Sunday school and in high school sang in the church choir. When I was very young Mother changed churches. My father's family had belonged to the Methodist church. Grandma Boyer, my father's mother, was a member of the WTCU, Women's Christian Temperance Union, I had heard. I think Mother decided that the Methodist church was too overbearing. She may have come to that conclusion after a couple of times when we were entertaining the minister which we did about once or twice a year and I remember one time just before he was to arrive in our home she went around the house checking to make sure all of the playing cards were put away. Playing cards? Playing cards are evil? I guess it's the gambling that the church was against. But our family played canasta and hearts with our playing cards, and I didn't think those were evil games. So we became members of the Congregational Church just up the street from the Methodist Church. In the early years we attended quite regularly and I went to Sunday school. Then as I became a teenager not so much. But most every Easter and every Christmas we were in church.

Our family didn't use alcohol; we had none in our home, except my father occasionally having some schnapps. My father smoked a pipe. So I, of course, was drawn to both alcohol and smoking cigarettes in my early teen years. I started with a bottle of vanilla and progressed from there to anything with alcohol in it. I do remember tasting my first beer and I hated it, but that didn't last long. When I was in high school, going to Oktoberfest was a rite of passage. And there were some nights when I was passed out in the back seat of a car.

Needless to say, my teen years were volatile while Robert stayed on track with good grades, was on the golf team, lettered in golf. He was indeed the good son, while I was continually getting into trouble as usual. He graduated from high-school and then applied at several colleges. After visiting some of these schools, he decided on Lawrence College in Appleton Wisconsin. I think he lasted a month or two, and then he came home and went to St Olaf College in Northfield Minnesota, just fifteen miles from home. I think he was just plain homesick; he missed his mother.

Now I don't know if Robert even knew at this point that he was gay; I doubt it. Gay men during the fifties were not accepted at all; in fact some called them queer. So if he did know, he likely kept it a secret, even from my mother. I do know that he never dated in high school or college that I was aware of. There was a girl in high school who was interested in him and called him often, and I remember one time Mother saying to him "Ginelle is on the phone, don't you want to talk with her?" He never did. I don't know what Mother knew or when she knew it. Likely she didn't face it until he declared it in the late seventies, but I will talk more about that later.

So he graduated from college in the usual four years, and because the draft was in effect, he had to serve his time in the military; as all young men did unless you were special and had someone in Congress or higher up to get a deferment for you. Or if you had some physical disability, you wouldn't have to serve. He went to Fort Gordon Georgia and Mother was terribly worried about him. In fact during boot camp, he became quite ill and was hospitalized with pneumonia. It seems to me Mother had intervened somehow through a friend who had a friend in higher places, to make sure he was properly taken care of. He survived. He became a Sargent with a desk job for the next two years. We flew to Atlanta once to visit him, taking him with us to Key West Florida for a short vacation.

Eventually his two years were up. He hated the Army, I could tell. When came home, he got rid of his uniform and never talked about that time again. He said many years later that during this time he had been sexually attacked when he was showering one day. What an awful experience for him.

He came home to Faribault and got a job as a history teacher at a private school where my mother had worked as a secretary during the time after she was divorced. And even when we moved out of our family home in Faribault, when my mother remarried and moved to Waseca, Robert rented a room, likely his old bedroom, in that house for a couple of years.

The story of my teen years is quite different. When I was eleven years old, I started to bleed from my vagina. I remember the day clearly like it was yesterday. I didn't know what was happening to me; I thought I was injured and hoped it would go away, but it didn't so I told my mother. Her response was not good. It was like "this is happening to you now, so soon, how awful". She found a menstrual period belt and showed me how to wear the menstrual pad. But there was no explaining why *this* was happening. And I hated it. I felt a seismic shift in my life, like it had changed forever and it had. It wasn't until I talked to friends at school that I found out what was happening to my body. I was in puberty. And I don't know how, but the boys knew it.

When I look back now, I was under siege from that time on. I was a pretty little girl and I was a lamb; I could easily be taken advantage of. And I didn't know how to handle it, because I had no one to teach me. I wasn't close to either my mother or my father. Mother seemed to be in her own world, depressed much of the time. She was seldom home; out shopping I guess or visiting friends. I was a latchkey kid without a key because she didn't trust me with one I guess. Many times I recall sitting on the back porch for hours after school waiting for her to come home and let me in the house. After a while I didn't come home. I found other places to be. When I searched through the papers and artifacts from the house, I think I found out why she was away from home so often, but I will also talk about that later in this story. And then when she divorced, she had to work.

I had a couple of incidences early on with men exposing themselves to me. In the winter when it was cold enough, the tennis court below the hill near our grade school was always flooded for a skating rink. It had a warming house and they piped music to skate with. When I was maybe four, I had received my first ice skates, the two runner type. I quickly graduated from those to the single blade figure skates. Then one Christmas when I was maybe twelve, I received a pair of good quality Canadian figure skates. I would spend every day, eight to ten hours during Christmas vacation at the skating rink. And I became quite proficient at skating. I could do all of the figures, I could do jumps. I loved skating to the music and would become completely lost in what I was doing so much so that I didn't pay attention to frozen toes and blisters on my heels. I just kept skating on. One evening when I was getting ready to go home—the rink was walking distance from my house—this guy offered me a ride. I knew him a little, had seen him at the rink often. It was a cold night so I said yes. I got into his car, he was much older than I was, and he drove me to my house and parked in front of it and turned off the motor. He unzipped his pants and exposed himself to me. I was shocked, and I immediately got out of the car. And I didn't know what to do. I couldn't tell my mother. She would be angry with me and likely punish me. I didn't even think to tell the police, and so I kept it to myself. I was so ashamed I didn't even tell a friend.

A year or so later it happened again. Somehow I became acquainted with this much older man. He was maybe twenty-five and had a farm. He also owned an airplane and invited me to go for a ride. Always the adventurer, I accepted. We flew over my house and did loops and dives, and I loved it. Sometime later he asked me to marry him. I was all of 14, and I laughed at him, and then he also exposed himself to me.

In school the teachers would always ask me if I was Robert's sister and of course I was. He was a hard act to follow. He excelled in all of his classes, and I am guessing the teachers expected me to be like him. But I wasn't.

Robert was a senior when I was in seventh grade. Junior and senior high school were combined at that time in our town, and there was only one public school. So Robert and I went to the same school for one year, and then he was off to college. Robert took it upon himself to introduce me to a friend of his who was a year ahead of me. His name was Lane, and he was one of the best looking boys in junior high so, even though I had yet to think of having a boyfriend, Robert hooked us up. Now, when I look back on this, my mother should have stopped this from happening, but she didn't. I was much too young to be dating. And when I think now about how Robert thought about me, he was probably hoping I would get pregnant. I guess that's being paranoid, but he never did anything for me out of the goodness of his heart. So I went to the movies with Lane and we went for walks and hikes. He kissed me a few times, but that was pretty much all that happened. I was an innocent and not ready for anything else and fortunately Lane wasn't expecting anything more than that. Oh, I was interested in boys; I had been since sixth grade. I and my girlfriends would talk about some of the boys we *liked*. I had my first kiss when I went to a slumber party at a girlfriend's house and later in the evening we invited some boys to join us. Her parents were gone. Again, why didn't my mother know what was happening? There was this one boy, with dark curly hair and big brown eyes. He took me to the bedroom and we sat on the bed and he kissed me. And that was it. But after that, he kept following me, and he would ride his bike to my house, sit in front and wait for me until Mother told him to go home. He even bought a bracelet and gave it to me, and Mother said I had to return it. I didn't know why.

So this early teen friendship with Lane was nothing more than that. However, I then became friends with his sister who was my age, and she took me to their house, which was in a very different part of town, below the hill, near the railroad tracks. It was more of a shack with no running water and an outhouse. I didn't know where their father was, and their mother of course was working. I lived in the better part of town in what was called Southern Heights.

Sharon and I became bosom buddies, our friendship continuing long after I stopped "going with" her brother. Sharon taught me some very bad habits. Now you might say I could have resisted, but again, ever up for something new, I went along with the program. She smoked cigarettes, drank liquor, went to bars and dance halls; it was a whole new world to me and so exciting. And she could do this because she looked a lot older than she was, had a well-developed female physique, more so than I did. And she had little or no parental supervision.

Again, where was my mother when I needed her most?

BATTLE OF THE WILLS

It was during this time that my father became very ill. He had a heart condition that the doctors determined would ultimately be fatal. They said that his childhood bout with rheumatic fever was likely the cause. He would not be able to carry on with his business. And with Robert starting college, these were terrible times for us. Our world was beginning to fall apart.

I hadn't heard for a week whether Gary had received the will, so I called over there and again talked with his administrative assistant. When I asked her about the will, she said they had received it, but because it was a copy and a bad one at that, it was not a valid will and would not hold up in court.

I was ecstatic. That meant that I would be able to inherit the estate. But then she said Gary had called Biron and they had gone to the house to try and locate the original will. "That will has to be someplace," she said.

"Good luck on that," I said. "I thoroughly searched that house for any and all wills that might be there. There are reams of paper to go through. It's going to take a while."

Then I said, "I don't think the original exists anymore. I think Robert tore it up after Jake left him. He would have been very angry with Jake, and that's what he would have done."

"Well, we'll have to wait and see."

I called Ray, my attorney, and gave him the update.

"How do they have access to the house? Didn't you change the locks when you were there?"

"I had intended to but when I heard from Jake that he had this will, I became distracted. I guess I should have."

And then I told him as well that I didn't think there was an original will and that Robert had destroyed it. "Biron told me that Robert had intended to write another will, but he may have gotten sick and never carried through with it."

"Except the holographic will that Biron wrote. And that's not a valid will," Ray said. "I guess we'll have to wait and see. I think you are right; Robert destroyed the original that Jake had."

Chapter Eight

It was in my early teen years that my family began to fall apart. Maybe before, but I wasn't aware. Mother was divorcing my father, and he had moved out of the house and was living with his mother. She had found a secretarial job and was gone even more than she had been before. So I was left to my own devices.

I was devastated that my parents were divorcing. I didn't understand it at all. Looking back from where I am now, I think I see what it was all about. My father had an incurable heart ailment and there were going to be thousands of dollars of medical bills; and no one had health insurance in the 1950's. And then there was the cost of Robert's college, with tuition probably about $1500 a year, which in those days was a chunk of money. Mother likely felt that they would be financially wiped out, so she took the nearest exit so to speak. There was no mortgage on the house, and if she had been a different person, she could have held the family together. But on the other hand, they could have lost the house if the medical bills were too high. It happens even today when people don't have health insurance and they have a catastrophic illness.

Divorce in those days was rare and not easy. One partner had to declare a reason for the divorce: infidelity or abusive behavior.

Today divorces are no-fault. In other words, one partner states they don't want to be married and they don't have to give a reason.

There was a court trial and there had to be a witness to the allegation. So I, all of maybe thirteen years old, was that witness. I shake my head. Again what was my mother thinking? I now barely remember this happening, I had suppressed these events; it was too painful to remember. And the "charges" of abuse, were of course all trumped up. It was a sham. If anyone was being abused, it was my father. I see that now. But I had no allegiance to either my mother or my father. I just wasn't close to either one of them. In fact, at that point in my life, I had no one to be close to. Yes, my grandfather, but he was far away and emotionally distant. That's the way many people were in those times I think.

Those last few years that they were together, even before my father's illness became apparent, their marriage was not a happy one. They seldom showed affection to one another; I don't ever recall seeing them kissing or hugging. I also think my father's business was faltering, maybe there was not enough money coming in. I recall Mother yelling at my father to collect on his overdue accounts. But the poor guy couldn't do everything. Why didn't she help him? But that's not what most women did in those days. She was the housewife. I think her parents were influencing her actions as well. I don't know this, but I think they always thought that my father was not good enough for my mother. They thought she could have done better.

But still, I don't understand it, and I think it was terribly wrong. She married for better or for worse. They'd been married for maybe twenty years. My father worked hard for her, built a house for the family, did the best he could.

As I mentioned earlier, divorce in those days was rare, and it was not condoned by society. So my friends kind of left me, and I found new friends, like Lane's sister. And I started to lead a different kind of life from what my former friends led.

Because Mother was working, I was on my own most of the time. I went to school and then came home to an empty house. I started hanging out in the Ice Cream Shop or some other restaurant downtown. I met a guy on a motorcycle. He was gorgeous, looked like James Dean. He took me for a ride on his cycle and we started hanging out together. It was an adventure. He was from Minneapolis and much older than I was. I did ask what he was doing in town, and he lied and said he and his buddy were there to paint houses. I found out later what they were really up to.

Every day after school he would pick me up and we'd go for a ride and then we went for walks. He kissed me and started pressuring me to have sex. I was a virgin and tried to resist. But he kept at me for maybe a month and finally I gave in. We went to my house; there was no one home. To my bedroom; and it was over in minutes. I remember the pain, and I really didn't like it.

I didn't see him again. Of course he knew that he could have been arrested for having sex with a minor, and he left town. But a couple of days later, our home was broken into. My mother came home and found the lock damaged on the back door, and I was not there, so she thought the worst, that I had been abducted. Nothing was taken, because we had few valuables in the house. But one of the thieves left a calling card on the garage floor. He defecated there.

I knew one of the sheriff's deputies. We were having a coke at one of my hangouts several days later and he told me that it was my motorcycle friend who had broken into our home. I look back on that and think about how he stole my virginity and then he broke into our home.

After Mother's divorce, Robert became the surrogate father during this time, even though he was away at college, which was only fifteen miles away. He came home most weekends and became the "man of the house."

I was trying to cope. I remember sometimes wishing I had never been born. But fortunately didn't act on it. I went to school, I played the flute and was in the band and that included marching band so we were in parades occasionally and played for the football games, sometimes going to neighboring towns. I remember staying late at school for band practice and walking home. The school was a mile away and up a hill to my house. It was in the fall. It was very dark that night, but I was never frightened to be walking alone at night. Then suddenly, two boys, they were kids, not adults, came rushing out of the bushes, pushed me down on the ground and started groping me. I screamed and they took off. I was so angry. When I got home, I told my mother, and the next day I went to the dean of women and told her about it. But of course I couldn't identify them, so nothing was done.

I had a regular babysitting job in the next block. The couple had three children, probably five, seven and a toddler. They were somewhat of celebrities. He was a well-known pro football player, and he married a young starlet. This gave me some extra spending money. I wanted to get an after school job, but Mother wouldn't allow it.

I hung out downtown more often now, and we, a couple of other girls and I would walk the main drag looking for boys. Yes, amazingly that's what we did. But, fortunately those were innocent times for the most part. A car with a couple of boys would pull up, ask if we wanted to go for a ride, we'd pile in, ride around for a while and that was that. Maybe we were lucky. But we did know these boys, and they never stepped out of line.

There was however a sexual predator in town. There may have been more than one, but I didn't know who they were. He in fact lived not too far from my house, and he drove a yellow Buick convertible and cruised the streets looking for young girls.

I was walking home from school one afternoon, and he cruised on by me, and then came back and asked if I wanted a ride home. I had seen him around. I loved convertibles, so I said yes and got into the car and he drove me home. Mother was not home of course. And then he started picking me up regularly and giving me rides. We sometimes would ride out in the country. He was about twenty five, very good looking; I thought he looked a little like Yul Brynner. He was married I found out. And then one afternoon he drove me out into the country and parked on a side road that seldom had traffic. He pulled me over to him and kissed me. I liked it. He asked me if I was a virgin, and I said no. And then he took me to the back seat of the car and we had sex. Consensual sex. He hadn't forced me, or raped me, I was a willing partner. And this "relationship" continued for maybe a year or more. I was all of fourteen years old. He would have been put in jail if the authorities had known. I, of course, was needy to say the least. I thought this was love. I don't know who knew about this, but my best friend, a schoolmate named, Lois, did know. Did my mother know? She never said anything or took any action. Fortunately, I didn't become pregnant.

It was about this time that Mother met a man from a nearby town. Robert actually facilitated this meeting. This man was an automobile dealer and Robert went there under the ploy of buying a car. He knew this man had lost his wife because the family was friends with my childhood friend, Jeanie. I had visited this man's house in fact with my friend and her parents several years ago.

So then Mother was dating? I couldn't believe it. But she was. She had lost some weight. She'd always been just a little bit overweight, and bought some flashy new clothes. This was not the mother I knew. And then he, the man, his name was Roy, showed up at our house—often. And it wasn't long before he asked her to marry him. And that Christmas, actually New Years, they were married in our church, with Robert and I and Roy's daughter, son-in-law with their daughter attending. I saw the photos again in among those that I had brought back from California. I wore a royal blue velveteen dress that I made myself. Yes, I loved to sew and made some of my own clothes. I remember just as they said their "I do's", I started bawling. My mother turned and glared at me. This was a seismic event in my life. I didn't know how this would play out, but I did know that I was about to be taken out of my childhood home and away from what friends I had left. But then also away from the predator. I didn't know it at the time but it was the best thing that could have happened to me.

I waited a day, and then I called Gary back again. Had they found a valid will? No, they hadn't. Robert dies in testate, and I was the only heir and would inherit Robert's estate, whatever that was. The house to be sure, if it was free and clear. But what would the medical liabilities be with him being so ill and having to be in a care facility and maybe having home care? And did he have any other investments or bank accounts? I didn't know.

I called Ray and told him and he said that we would file in probate the next day.

I was making plans to go back to California and prepare the house for sale. What a job that would be. I talked with Alan, my son, and he said that he might be able to come down for a couple of days to help out. I wanted to drive over because I knew I would be bringing more things back with me. To be sure the two chairs I had left at the neighbor's house. But I wasn't looking forward to this gig, even though there might be great financial gain for me.

What would I do with this money, if there would be a substantial amount after paying off creditors? I didn't need it. I was financially secure. I thought about maybe going to Redlands and living in the house. It was a much nicer house than the one I had owned for almost forty years. It had three bedrooms and two baths, while my house had one bathroom which was plenty for me. It had a garage, while my house had a carport. It had a fireplace, while mine had none, but I had chiminea's in the back yard, which was almost as good. The place had a walk-in closet in the master suite, Mother's bedroom. I had always wanted a walk-in closet. But the more I thought about it, the more I realized that I was not going to be leaving Phoenix to go and live in Redlands, even though the town was quaint and the people were nice. Phoenix was my home. I have friends there, my author's groups, my doctors, which are very important, and I'll tell you more about that later. But the clincher was that I would not be able to have my dogs there. The HOA doesn't allow large dogs and Sophie my weimaraner at seventy pounds would qualify for a large dog. There wasn't enough yard for them anyway.

Alan was encouraging me to stay in Phoenix, and I'm not sure why. Then Alan came up with the idea of using the money to buy a cabin in the woods, up on the Mogollon Rim in Arizona, Pinetop or Lakeside. Perfect, I thought. A place where I could escape the heat in the summer, bring the dogs, let them chase deer, and I could go skiing in the winter. So that was one plan. And then should I bring the furniture back to Phoenix and store it until I got a cabin? That was a possibility. Many options were available.

Chapter Nine

The next Sunday I was off again on the road to Redlands. I had contacted LuAnn my pet sitter to come and stay with the girls, Sophie and Lily, telling her that I would be home by Thursday at the latest. She had stayed with them the last trip and did a good job, so I wouldn't have to worry about them.

I was planning on leaving on Monday, but had an email from Jerry the Treasurer for the HOA inviting me to the monthly meeting at 2 p.m. on Sunday, so I thought why not leave a day early and go and meet the neighbors. If I left Phoenix at 8 a.m., I should get in by a little after noon and I gain an hour due to change in time zones. So that's what I did. And I thought there might be less traffic on Sunday, maybe fewer trucks on I-10, a road that I have come to despise. This highway was built in the 60's and may have been entirely adequate then, but fifty years later, the road can barely handle the amount of traffic traveling east and west. It is a four lane road, two lanes west and two east with soft shoulders and few pull off areas. The speed limit in Arizona is 75 miles per hour and 70 in California and you just about have to keep up with the flow; which is five miles over the speed limit most times, 80 miles per hour. And the right lane is really bumpy due to the trucks using this lane most of the time so it is better to stay in the left lane most of the time. After I returned from the last trip I heard that two women were killed on this road. I will do the best I can. I am rested and alert.

I put the big box in the back of my Element again, planning on bringing back many items. I packed a light lunch, filled my water bottle, and I was off pretty much on schedule. There was a lot of traffic going out of town, but it let up some as I reached Tonopah, and the drive across the desert was uneventful. I was soon in Blythe filling my tank, and then drove on into Redlands arriving at 12:30. I brought my bag into the house and put it in the bedroom. Then I had some time to look around the house and rest before the meeting. Things were pretty much as I had left them when I was last here.

At two, I walked over to the pool area where people were gathered. I introduced myself and found a chair to sit in. Later in the meeting, I was asked if I would be moving into the house, and I said no, that I was there to prepare the home for sale. I told them I loved Redlands but my home was in Phoenix, and I think they understood.

After the meeting, I went to the grocery store and bought a six pack of beer and some hot dogs. I had brought some food with me and I had intended to use any non-perishable, canned or frozen food in the house that I could. I hate wasting food.

I came home and had a beer, cooked a hot dog in the microwave and opened a can of baked beans. That was my supper. This was my meal for several more nights. There were some little prepared puddings in the refrigerator and I ate one of those. It wasn't very good, but it was something sweet.

I went to bed early, taking my book about birds to read. For some reason, I felt entirely comfortable being in the house alone, not like the last time when I was, I can't say frightened, but just on edge. I fell asleep easily. There was going to be a lot of hard work ahead of me in the week ahead. My mother and Robert had been living in this house since 1982, and it was still full of stuff, although most of my mother's clothing and personal things were gone, except a few pieces of costume jewelry. I guess Robert had to make room for Jake.

I woke the next morning on Arizona time, about 6 a.m. I made some coffee and tried to prepare some toast, but the toaster wasn't working. I found some frozen Jimmy Dean sausage and muffins and put one in the microwave. I stirred some Emergen-c into a glass for my orange juice.

After drinking a cup of coffee, I started to work beginning with a mental inventory of everything in the house. There was the clothing in Robert's and the hall closet. The huge linen closet running the length of the hallway was full of linens and towels and many other items as well. It looked like a catch-all when they didn't know what to do with something. I have some of that at home as well. And the kitchen cupboards were full of dishes and pots and pans and bakeware. There was some food, canned goods, pasta, and spices which I would use or take with me. The pantry was full of more dishes, crystal, more knick-knacks, and other stuff, like candles and artificial flowers. Then there was the furniture: two beds, two dressers, three end tables, one desk, one three drawer metal file cabinet full of papers, consisting of mostly copies of law suits, one occasional chair in the bedroom and another in the living room, one love seat that was my grandmothers, two lazy boys, one of which will have to be taken to the dump as it is trashed, one hide-a-bed, three book cases full of books, one large yellow sofa that was like new because Mother kept a cover on it and seldom allowed people to sit on it, except the dog, one dining room set with five ladder-back chairs and one yellow wrought iron patio table with four matching chairs in the kitchen. Oh, and then two analog TV sets, that no one would want. I still wondered why Robert hadn't upgraded to digital and he had no computer. I don't even know if he had a cell phone. He appeared to be living back in the last century.

Then there was the garage which was full of a lot of trash, a pile of old car radios, a bunch of wheel mounts, stacks of papers, one bicycle, an exercise bicycle, an artificial Christmas tree, and one automobile. There were cupboards full of gardening supplies, and who-knows-what-else. The garage alone would take a day to clean. The back patio needed to be cleaned, the grass trimmed and the roses cut back. Thursday… I was leaving on Thursday? Not looking good. *Maybe I need some help. Alan isn't coming after all. He's busy with work.*

The plumber showed up about 8 a.m. to fix the shower and attach the new shower heads that I had brought. I had called him from Arizona before I left because I knew the shower wasn't working. He charged me way too much money. I called Jaun, the gardener and Robert's caregiver for a time, and he came right over. I think he was already in the neighborhood. We talked about the automobile, and I had misplaced the title to the car, so I might have to go to DMV and get a duplicate. I wasn't sure how to transfer the car as Robert had already started this transaction, but I guess he became too ill to finish it. He had wanted Juan to have the car as partial payment for his caregiving services.

Then I took Juan out to the garage and asked if he could haul off the trash and also clean the back yard and trim the bushes in front and he said he would come back tomorrow with his truck to haul the trash and then work on the yard. He was charging me $250.00, and that seemed reasonable to me. Juan works hard and he seems trustworthy.

I called Rita, the real estate agent that I had contacted last week, and she said she could meet with me in the afternoon. I was anxious to meet her and find out if we were compatible working together. I had half a dozen agents calling me, emailing, sending me literature, comps on the house and market plans. But Rita said the right words to me when I first talked with her. She told me that she worked hard to sell a property, in staging it and marketing it and the goal was to get the highest price possible. Those were the right words.

I called my attorney and told him I was in town. He said he didn't need to see me but if I needed help with anything he would be available. I then called Biron, and he told me he would come over later.

It was almost noon by the time I got started actually getting some closets cleaned out. I had brought some boxes and bags and got those out to use. I started loading my car with clothing from Robert's closet. As I put the clothes in the car, I recognized some of it and memories again came flooding back. I needed to give them to a thrift shop, and I was hoping Rita would know which one would be good for taking these things. And then I started putting all of the crystal out on the dining table, carefully wrapping each piece in newspaper, and putting them in a box that I had brought. Then the dishes. I would have to stop by Home Depot and pick up more packing boxes.

Biron stopped by, and I was glad to see him. We sat and talked for a while, and then I went back to wrapping and packing up dishes and things. Biron mentioned dinner for tomorrow evening, and I thought that would give me a little break. He left soon after. I started pulling towels and linens out of the biggest linen closet I have ever seen. How could two people have this many towels and wash cloths? And sheets and table linens? But when people have the storage space, they tend to fill it. I know, I am one of those.

Rita stopped by in the early afternoon, and we sat and talked for about an hour. I really liked her energy, and she had some good ideas for marketing the house. I then asked her about thrift shops where I could take things. After she left, I took a load of clothing to Goodwill and stopped by the grocery again. By the time I got back "home", my home away from home, it was dinner time. I had hardly made a dent in getting things cleaned out, but there was always tomorrow.

I went for a walk after dinner, and then came back and fell into bed with my book.

Juan came over as I was having breakfast. He started right in on the garage, loading the back of his truck with all the stuff. We began looking through the cupboards, throwing some of it away, and I told Juan to take the things he could use. Then Juan pulled down some old boxes from the top shelves of the cupboards along the side of the garage. I opened them and one had more old photographs and letters and the other was a mish-mash of papers, Robert's and my school papers and other little mementos from our childhood. I took these boxes into the house, and sat on the yellow sofa that I was not allowed to sit on when Mother was alive. I thought about how, if I had not been able to come back and clean this house out, those photos and mementos would have been lost forever.

We finished cleaning the garage about noon, ahead of schedule, and then Juan worked on the patio area, trimming back the grass and the roses, and he trimmed the bushes in front to make things look neater. Once done with the yard, he went home.

I took more clothes to the Assistance League thrift shop in Redlands. Salvation Army came and picked up some of the furniture. I had talked with a woman on Monday who said she would inventory all the furniture and make me an offer on the better pieces that she would take to her consignment store and sell, and I thought that was a good idea. I had decided early on not to have an estate sale. For one thing I didn't want to have strangers going through the home, and I also felt that you seldom make very much money on this type of sale. I had looked into taking some of the better pieces home with me in case I would buy a cabin, but it was too costly, and then I would have to store them, costing even more money. If I did buy a cabin, I could buy some really nice furniture from the thrift stores in Phoenix.

Biron came over and we went to dinner at the Sizzler. I had a small steak, I normally don't eat meat, but I thought I needed the protein, and a salad. When we finished, he drove me back to the house and left me there and it was early to bed again.

The next day more of the same. I signed the papers to list the house. Rita said that I was making great progress. I guess; I had filled two more trash cans and taken several loads of clothing, dishes and linens to the thrift shop. Tomorrow was Thursday, and there was no way that I could leave now. I had to finish this job. I texted LuAnn and told her that it would be Friday when I got home. But truthfully I didn't know if that would happen either. I wanted to go home. I missed my dogs. I was lonely having to do this mostly by myself; it was a huge job. And I was emotionally thinking about all of the time I had spent in this house and how I hated to come here, but I guess I did it out of duty to my mother. I recalled when she was first starting to become ill; she'd asked me to come and live here. I think at that point she was afraid of being abused by Robert. But I couldn't do that. I had a good job in computing; I was making money and socking a lot away for my retirement so that I would have enough. I told Mother that. I don't think she understood. But I knew the neighbors and they were looking in on her and Robert, so I thought they would tell me if I needed to do anything different. And then someone asked, why doesn't you mother come and live with you? But she never would have come to Phoenix. She would never leave Robert and she hated Phoenix.

More cleaning out cupboards and closets. Getting rid of the papers in the file cabinet. Rita took some of the old towels to the animal shelter, and they were grateful. I donated the bicycle to the bike shop; they said they refurbish older bikes and donate them to kids who can't afford to buy them.

It's Friday and I'm still not done. I see another full day of work. I text LuAnn and tell her Sunday for sure. She said she couldn't stay past Sunday, so I will be forced to go home.

The Salvation Army comes for a second time to pick up more furniture and some boxes of stuff and bags of clothing. I take some of the last bags of linens and things to the thrift shop, and on the way back, I fill my tank in preparation for my trip home. When I got home, I checked every room to see if I had missed anything. I looked under Robert's bed and found a bunch of gay porn magazines. Like he had hidden them from Mother. It was almost too funny, but they were really gross. I had found many porn books and tapes in the bookcases. I am not a prude, but I thought, what a waste of time. I loaded them into the trash bin in the garage as I had done with all of the porn materials I had found that week.

I then started to load the car with the things I would be taking with me; the two little maple chairs, the big box of family photos and other stuff, some more paintings.

Throughout the week as I had been removing all of my family's belongings from the house, I felt my mother looking over my shoulder, and I wondered what she would think about what

I was doing. No doubt she would not approve as I was literally giving these things away, and she would not like that at all. But then she seldom approved of what I did; I don't' recall hearing words of praise from her for much of anything. My thoughts are that used household goods and furnishings are worth very little money. If someone else was able to use and enjoy them, then I had accomplished what I intended. My one goal was to try to keep these things out of the land fill.

I have supper, and then go for my last walk in Redlands. I will likely never come back here again. That's always a sad thought, even though my visits were almost always painful and full of unhappiness. But this is another phase in my life. My family, although very small, is gone, except for my son, whom I seldom see any longer, because he is far away, very busy working and can't visit that often.

I will never see these mountains again, or the orange groves. But it is time to put this all behind me and get on with my life. I have to remember that I have made a very good life for myself in Phoenix.

Chapter Ten

I had planned on leaving at eight, but it was going on 9 a.m. on Sunday, and I am just now pulling onto the freeway. There has been a light rain and the glare of the sun on the wet road is really bad, but I take my time. Soon I am coming into the Palm Springs area. I glanced over at San Jacinto, likely for the last time, drove past Indio, and then I am climbing the grade out of the valley to the high desert. I think back to the time I made this trip, the day after Mother's funeral in 1999. I had stayed overnight with Robert against my son's wishes. He was concerned Robert might try to harm me. He remembered my telling him about the incident a year or so before she died, when I had come to visit Mother after she'd had her stroke. I had flown into Ontario, and Robert came to pick me up. The next day we went to visit Mother in the nursing home. The nurse brought her out in a wheel chair, and she barely recognized me. That evening Robert took me to dinner up into the mountains outside Redlands. On the way home, Robert started to pull off the highway and turn down a narrow gravel road. I asked him where he was taking me, and he said we were going to look at some blueberries. Blueberries? There weren't any blueberries down there, and we were alone. I freaked out. I started opening the car door and told him I wouldn't go there, and then he laughed a funny laugh and got back on the main road. I was truly afraid that he was going to kill me. After that, I never flew to California, I always drove so that I could be in control.

The afternoon of the day of the funeral, after the services, Robert and I were walking around the complex and we met a neighbor. I think she was a doctor. We talked about the funeral, and Robert said he was going to sue and the woman gave him funny look and asked why. As did I. What a strange thing to say. Mother was 88 years old. She'd had a stroke and was near a vegetable. Why would he sue?

When I arrived home and for the next few weeks and months I didn't much think about it until one day at work, a process server came to our office looking for me. I didn't know why that would be until he pressed this large envelope of papers in my hand and said "you have been served." What? Served? For what, I wondered. I hadn't been served since I had my first divorce in 1978. I went to the break room and opened the envelope, and I was dumbstruck. It was a lawsuit naming Mother's doctor, the hospital, the nursing facility where she had been cared for and *me*. He's suing me? Unbelievable. I read on and the allegations were that the doctors and the hospital and care facility had incorrectly administered her medication. The suit was alleged I had killed my mother. How could that be? How could I kill my mother from Arizona even if I wanted to? Which of course I didn't.

Then I thought back to that last time that I visited her in the hospital and how I'd said that it was time to let her go. She couldn't eat, didn't recognize us, and couldn't even talk. She wore a diaper and that had to have been embarrassing for her. When I left to go home, Robert screamed at me, "You want to kill your mother."

I think he had planned this for a long time. I don't really know of course. But when Mother first was having dementia, Robert uncharacteristically became my best friend. I took it at face value and was pleased that for the first time in my life I had a brother. But then when she was very ill and in the nursing home, he turned on me. I should have expected that, knowing how he had treated me all of his life, but I was naïve.

I was devastated. I called a friend that evening, a lawyer whom I had dated several years ago and told him about the law suit against me. His first words were, "That motherfucker". He wanted me to come to his office and he said he would help me. I was thankful to have him as a friend.

The next day I went to my attorney friend's office, he took me to his conference room and we sat down. I gave him the documents, and he perused them for a while, shaking his head. He said I would have to get an attorney in California. I explained that Mother's trust named Robert as executor. Because he'd been dragging his heels in settling everything, I had hired my own attorney who specialized in estates and trusts. According to the trust that my mother had set up at my brother's insistence, I was to get half my mother's estate which was fair. And because she had the trust, the estate would not go through probate.

"You will need another attorney that handles criminal cases," he said. "Obviously your brother wants all of the estate and he wants to ruin you with having to pay thousands in attorney's fees." He then told me that my homeowners insurance would pay for this law suit—if I was not guilty. And of course, I wasn't. The way I saw it, it was a frivolous lawsuit. How could I possibly have killed my mother; I was in Arizona. I had little contact with her or her doctors. He was the one who managed her care. To say that that I was angry at Robert is an understatement, but I was also angry with the sleazy law firm that agreed to this case.

For three years, we haggled. I went to a deposition in California. And then we fought some more, but finally Robert settled, giving me my half of the estate. Which was half of her cash holdings and investments, and he had to pay me for my half of the house. The house that I am now inheriting. It was after that that I decided I didn't want him in my life anymore. He only wanted to harm me. After he told me that I had to pay for my baby pictures—that was it. I was done with him. My life would be better without him in it. And that was very true. I had thirteen years of happiness, with the exception of my five years with cancer, but I'll tell you about that later.

So after fighting for it, I received my half of my Mother's estate. And of course I took that money and invested it wisely, whereas he obviously spent his half. And my homeowners insurance paid for my attorney' fees, which came to $25,000.

What Robert didn't know, though, was that before Mother had the trust, which he encouraged her to do, she had a will written years before. I found this will when I was going through some old papers in the house. In that will she left everything to Robert and stated that he should give me whatever he thought was fair. You and I know what that would have been. Nothing. So here is another example of how my mother favored Robert. And, unbelievably, I wasn't that aware of this. Nor did I care in fact. I just wanted to get away. Away from her and away from Robert, and yet I kept being drawn back in, I guess because I felt an obligation to them. They were my family; all the family I had, except later on my son. But no more.

My living room is full. The big box sitting in the middle, with other old boxes of papers and books and mementos spread out everywhere. For about a week, I just looked at it and didn't know where to start. I couldn't possibly keep all this stuff. But I couldn't throw it away either. This was my family history. And as bad as it was, I wanted to know more about it and perhaps preserve some of it. I had other projects to work on. My manuscript was ready to go to my editor and I had bills to pay, a house to take care of and the dogs. But then I set aside a little time every afternoon to sort through the mess. I found my Mother's high school diploma, an essay she had written and won an award for. There were my and Robert's grade school papers. I was amazed at how neatly I wrote in cursive, little poems and essays. My grades were excellent before I got to high school.

I opened a box tied with a ribbon and found love letters from my father to my mother. They weren't all that mushy; he called her "dear child". He wrote mostly about his daily activities and how he was starting his business. He said he missed her but never really said "I love you". I was not clear why he was writing to her. The postmark on the envelopes was 1933, they were married, and it appeared that she had gone home to be with her parents. Maybe she was pregnant with Robert and needed to be with her mother. It was kind of strange.

I found their marriage certificate. The story Mother told me was that when she and my father went to her parents to tell them they were getting married, she was rebuffed by her parents and told to leave the house. Why, I don't know. Could have been that my grandparents didn't want to pay for a wedding. They were like that. Or maybe they didn't approve of my father. Certainly that was a mean-spirited thing to do if it was true—but it was hearsay.

Mother was an only child. He parents did everything for her, and I think all of her life she felt inadequate. Everything was difficult for her. She had two children, not a big family for sure, but she was always behind on everything. She was a homemaker most of her life, but she hated cleaning the house, doing laundry, and the daily drudgery of keeping a home. To be fair, she didn't have modern appliances like we have today. The old wringer washer was in the basement, and she had to carry wet baskets of clothing up the basement stairs and hang the clothes on a clothesline when weather permitted. In the winter the clothes were hung in the basement.

There was no dishwasher; dishes and pot and pans were washed in the sink and dried with a dish towel. As we got older we had to help out, which was a good thing. I always tried to get out of doing any housework, however. Mother occasionally hired a house keeper and sent the laundry out.

When she remarried—by that time we had the modern appliances—she had a regular house keeper every week. Her name was Evelyn. Mother would clean the house before Evelyn came because, she didn't want her to see how dirty things were.

As I sorted through the papers, I found something else that struck me as being odd. There were many photos, letters and other mementos, along with newspaper articles about her doctor. This was the doctor that delivered both my brother and me. He also performed the surgery on her to repair her female organs after I was born. He was a small town doctor and had an office in his home, but he also did research and had made a name for himself in the larger medical community. In fact, I looked him up on the internet and there was information about him.

I thought back to those many days when Mother was gone for long afternoons. And I looked at the memorabilia she had collected about her doctor and the little books and things he had given her. I won't give his name here for obvious reasons. I remember going to his home; he was married and we were invited for coffee one time.

I think she was in love with him. She may never have had a physical relationship with him, but she might have wished she had married someone like him. He was an intellectual and loved literature as she did. Whereas my father was a more of the engineer type, designing things, a whiz at math, and maybe not a romantic. They were a mismatch, and she probably knew it then. But I think she may have married my father to escape a terribly unhappy home life. And so, ironically the cycle repeats itself. This is exactly what I had been doing most of my life; escaping.

After Mother remarried, she moved into her new husband's home in a nearby town, and then after a few months, I had to go and live with her. I didn't want go. This was the only life I knew and I was afraid of leaving the small number of friends I had. But a few weeks into January of that year, Mother sent Robert to literally drag me out of school and pack a few things for the move. I cried. But there wasn't much I could do.

I remember that next week, my stepfather, Roy took me to the new high school and introduced me to the principle. I was all of fifteen years old and this was the middle of my junior year. I was so frightened.

I also remember going to the first assembly in the auditorium, sitting there, not knowing anyone. Someone clasped my shoulder behind me. I turned around, and there was this boy sitting there looking at me.

"You're new here," he said. "My name's Ken. After the assembly, let me introduce you to some friends."

What a kind thing for him to do, and we became good friends. I was on my way to having new friends in my new school. My life was looking up.

In the next year and a half, my grades turned around, I went to slumber parties and other events that normal teenagers do. I had a new steady boyfriend, who was truly in love with me and me with him—puppy love. I have to give much of the credit to my new stepfather who understood how to deal with a difficult teen.

One evening he sat me down on the sofa and had a little talk with me. He told me about how I had two different paths ahead of me and my choices would decide what kind of life I would have; one was the path I had been on, a path of self-destruction and the other was the path to a successful, happy life. I had to choose now which one I would take. I remember that talk to this day; I get goosebumps thinking about it. But it had an impact on me. I think I always wanted to be on the right path, but I needed help, I needed a rudder, someone who cared and he was the one who gave it to me.

My boyfriend asked me to the prom that spring, and I was so excited. Mother took me to Minneapolis to buy a special dress, but the weekend of the prom Mother and Roy went to Hawaii. I was crushed. I wanted her to be there on this important day, but my grandparents came and filled in for her.

I graduated from high school that next spring and was told that I would be going to college in the fall, the school that Robert had attended, St. Olaf College. I had never been told that before, so I wasn't exactly prepared for college. My grades were not good enough; the school only accepted those in the upper ten percent of their class. I was far away from that. Because Robert had gone before me, the school made an exception, but I had to take a test. I passed the test and received the letter that summer that I was accepted.

It was about this time that Robert had a bad automobile accident in Waseca where Mother and I were living with Roy. He hadn't completely stopped at a stop sign and collided with another car. He had head injuries, a broken jaw and lost several of his front teeth. After that he had to have a partial plate of false teeth for the rest of his life. I don't know if they had dental implants in 1958. But I think it had quite an effect on him. He also was becoming bald by this time, inheriting this from our father. Robert was quite vain and I think this bothered him as well.

I had a job that summer after high school graduation, working for a small manufacturing company in town. My boyfriend's father got the job for me. I was an expeditor, looking for lost invoices. It was sometimes interesting and challenging, but mostly boring. I think I earned all of $350 for the three months that I worked there. I spent the whole amount on—a Singer sewing machine, the deluxe model that did special stiches. Mother was livid that I had spent all of my money on this sewing machine. But I was going to college and my major would be Home Economics being especially interested in clothing construction and design. It made sense to me that I would have this deluxe model of a sewing machine. But again that was Mother; she never approved of very much that I did. Ironically I still have that sewing machine today and I use it mainly for mending things.

Before starting school that fall, Mother took me to Minneapolis to buy clothes for college, an amazing wardrobe, including a faux fur coat. Now when I look back, I see the purpose of my going to school; to get my MRS degree. I guess Mother wanted to be rid of the responsibility of having a daughter.

The first year of college went well. I lived in the freshman dormitory and had two roommates. I went to all my classes and attended the social functions. We were required to go to chapel every day; St. Olaf is affiliated with the Lutheran Church. To be honest, I skipped chapel most of the time. The college had very strict rules: no dancing, no smoking or drinking, all of the things I did. Oh, but because these activities were not allowed, we found other things to do: blanket parties. I think dances would have been a better activity. And in addition, no automobiles allowed on campus. But many broke that rule.

On week nights, if we went out, we had to be back in the dorm by 10:30 p.m. and on weekends by 11:30, and the house mother was always at the door, monitoring us, I'm sure smelling our breath for alcohol. As freshmen, we were not allowed to go home for the weekend, only on holidays. But I was an innovator. When Robert was at college there, my grandparents had moved to Northfield, where the college is located, to give him more support. They bought a little home just below the college; St. Olaf is on a hill. So I would tell my house mother that I was spending the weekend with my grandparents. Then with some of my friends, we'd pile into a car and drive up to the University of Minnesota and go to frat parties. I only did that a couple of times. One of the times, I remember, we packed an old Volkswagen Beetle with about eight people and drove on ice all the way. But those little cars were really good in icy conditions.

Also it just so happened that Grandma's neighbor was the dean of women at the college and they were good friends. That was a benefit.

I was put on probation in my second year. My grades were not good. I did well in most classes, but I failed chemistry, a class I needed for my field of study. Again looking back, I was not prepared for this school. I had little or no math skills, which I needed for the chemistry class. And I did not have good study habits. I should never have been sent to this college; I would have done better at a state teachers college. The goals set for me were not graduation, they were to find a husband and hopefully a wealthy one. And, in retrospect, because I had little self-discipline, Mother may have thought that the strict rules of the school would keep me in line. It didn't. I still smoked, going off campus to a small café at the bottom of the hill, which took a lot of time. I still drank on weekends. And my high school boyfriend was there, so I was still having sex. And then I dumped him and started dating another guy, whom I dated for the next couple of years. Should have married him. But he's still in Wisconsin, and I wouldn't want to be there.

One incident stands out in my mind during that time. I think in my second year at St. Olaf, one afternoon I was walking up the hill from the café, and the yellow Buick convertible from my past pulled up beside me and stopped. He rolled down the window and beckoned to me, and I went over to talk with him. He told me to get inside the car. I just looked at him and said, "No, I can't do that anymore." As he drove away I wondered, was he here looking for me? Or was he just trolling for another victim. I will never know. But I had grown in stature that day.

BATTLE OF THE WILLS

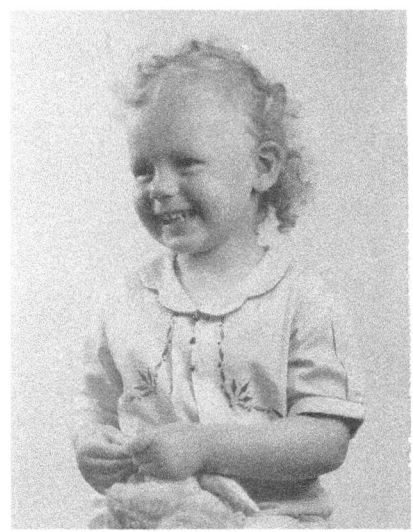

Robert was a happy toddler

Mother and Robert dressed for winter

Above: Elaine in baby buggy

Right: Dad with Elaine and Robert

Robert at 2 years

Elaine in pink bonnet, age three

Elaine at fourteen

Baby Elaine in high chair

Mother, Father and Elaine by spruce tree

Seeing Uncle Harlan off to World War II – 1943

BATTLE OF THE WILLS

Father – Stanley Boyer

Great Grandma Hannah Franklin

Maternal grandparents

Mother when she was a young woman

Mother, Robert, Elaine and neighbor at Robert's Lake

Elaine, Robert and Mother at Glacier Park

Elaine with muff and Robert with 1942 Plymouth

Childhood home built by father

Seeing Uncle Harlan off to World War II

BATTLE OF THE WILLS

Elaine in charity fashion show

Elaine and Warren's wedding February 17, 1962

Elaine and Jon Wedding May 24, 1985

Elaine, Alan Grandma and Grandpa – Warren, Robert and Mother

Elaine Mays

Alan and Me when I first
had cancer

Mother in back yard with flowers

Alan and Mother when she was 85

Chapter Eleven

Thanksgiving was fast approaching and I was determined to get the "past" out of my living room. The house in California had sold, even before it hit the market, and at full price. Rita had known what I knew all along; the property was unique. Homes in this complex seldom came up for sale and so there were people waiting for that to happen. Because it was an end unit and there were orange grove across the street, it had a unique isolation, providing privacy that the other units didn't have. The house was also in surprisingly good shape. Robert had taken good care of it. He had replaced the AC and had the interior painted. I saw a handwritten bill for the painting, and I couldn't believe my eyes; the amount was $22,000. Did he really pay that? If so, he got ripped off royally. I'll know more when I look at his bank accounts.

I was both happy and sad, however. Every home is personal, holding family memories. Even though they might not have the best memories, they hold an integral part of you and your history. I know that to be true of the house I live in now. I bought my home in 1978 when I was first divorced. It is a small home, but it is warm and friendly, and I often say that my house hugs me; it is my safe haven, even though I live in the middle of a big city with crime all around me. That was what I wanted for my mother and brother: a safe haven. And they had that. But I don't think they appreciated what they had. Living in such a beautiful, crime free and quiet area, this small picturesque town, where the weather is almost always sunny and the people equally friendly. It was paradise. I think they blew it off with their petty grievances and resentment of life in general. I am sorry for both of them. I refuse to let negativity cloud my life. I embrace life. As I like to say, I always have fun. If you can't have fun, what is there left in life?

But then Robert was not well, and I don't think Mother was either. She was the epitome of enablers, and they fed off each other. I tried once or twice talking to her about it, but she wouldn't listen to me, and she wouldn't hear anything negative about Robert. So I stopped. There was nothing I could do. I tried to love them and be supportive at a distance.

I picked through the myriad of greeting cards that I had sent to Robert and Mother over the years: Christmas cards, birthday cards, Mother's Day cards, Easter and even Valentine's Day. They had saved everything. I sent Christmas presents every year, trying to pick out something they would like and they were returned to me. So I stopped doing that.

I do think Robert was feeding her information about me that wasn't true, poisoning her mind. As I look back, I believe he was doing that all along. Probably when I was a teen telling her that I was wild and having sex. Mother thought sex was dirty. And so if she thought that I was having sex, I was a dirty person.

The reason I say this because we never talked about sex. Ever. One time when I was married, I went to spend some time with her in California to heal my soul after losing my third child, and Mother for the first time in my life was trying to help me. I was there without my husband, Warren. After a month, he came to join me. Mother put him in a separate bedroom away from me.

She wasn't going to have that sex thing going on in her house even though we were married. Too funny now when I think of it. Warren came to my bed anyway.

After failing at St. Olaf College, I went back to Waseca and got a job with a local insurance company doing menial tasks, filing and taking care of the mail. I knew I had to move on. There was no future here for me, so I decided to go back to school and I chose Winona State College in Winona, Minnesota. The picturesque town is located on the Mississippi River and the school was small. I decided that I wanted to be a teacher majoring in Elementary Education, thinking teaching young children would be a great and noble thing to do. Until I was asked to substitute teach at the college campus kindergarten. Those kids ran circles around me, and I seriously thought that this wasn't the career for me.

I had a boyfriend. His name was Curt and he was a big, affable Norwegian who came from the farm. He played the piano on weekends in the local bars to help pay for school. He was a fun-loving guy, and I enjoyed being around him.

I stayed in the girls dormitory, had a roommate and my grades were good. I could easily keep up with this class schedule.

One evening I was studying when a friend came into my room and said I had a phone call. I went to the pay phone that we all shared, and it was my mother calling to say that my father had died. I asked if I could go to the funeral, but she said his family had already had the funeral. She said she wasn't notified either; she saw the notice in the paper. I was devastated. I couldn't even say goodbye to my father.

I turned 21 that spring. I went out with my boyfriend to a bar, now that I could legally drink, but the bartender wouldn't believe I was of age. I had a baby face and looked very young, so I had to carry my driver license with me when I went out. On my birthday

Mother never even called. But what I didn't know was that she was divorcing my stepfather, or he was divorcing her, don't know which. It had to do with his family who were concerned that she would inherit from him and they would not get their fair share. They had a prenuptial when they married. My stepfather had a considerable amount of money, but as it turned out, it wasn't legal, because he had presented the prenup to her the night of the wedding, and it would not hold up in court. His daughter who lived in Waseca was the one who discovered this and likely pressured her father into divorcing my mother.

This changed everything. I now had no money for school. And Mother had no place to live. I think she was fifty and had no work history. Although after attending Hamlin University where she met my dad, she had gone to secretarial school.

That May when school ended, I was homeless. But my boyfriend came to my rescue and offered refuge at his nearby farm home, and I accepted. I was given a small closet like room on the top floor of this old farmhouse. I helped his mother, who was very nice, but very quiet, with the cooking. It was fun. We shelled peas and prepared other fresh vegetables for dinner. I loved being on the farm, but I was worried where I would go from there. I couldn't stay forever.

Mother had gathered her belongings, put them in storage I guess and went to Minneapolis, staying in a hotel room for a time. It was at this time that she met Sam, who was in town from San Bernardino for the Shriner's convention. He invited her to the fancy dress ball. She rented a dress she told me. He was a 32nd degree Freemason, pretty high up in this secret organization.

Obviously they became friends, although he was married. But his wife, he told her, was an invalid. It was Sam who talked Mother into coming to California, and I think he helped her get established there. Which she needed.

BATTLE OF THE WILLS

In the meantime, I was hanging out on the farm not knowing what I would do, when Robert came up with a solution. North West Airlines was hiring stewardesses, and he thought I should apply. And I did. I traveled to Minneapolis and Robert took me to the North West offices; Minneapolis was their home base. I wore a cute little mint green dress. My hair was cut short, and I paid special attention to my nails and makeup. I remember the interview, a kind of stern-looking woman asking me if I liked working with people and some other questions. I was the right age; you had to be twenty-one. I walked out of her office into the waiting room and was told to sit down. Minutes later a woman approached me and told me that I was hired. That was easy.

In retrospect, I think Robert was hoping that, when I got the job, my airplane would go down and I would be killed and out of his life. And I know this sounds like I am paranoid, but he never did anything kind for me; he always had an agenda.

They gave me the address of where I would be staying during my six week training period. It was an old hotel downtown. It was dirty and dreary and within a couple of days, all the trainees lobbied for better accommodations. And it was then that they found this new apartment complex in Bloomington, south Minneapolis. It had four large, two story buildings placed around an inner court yard with a pool and was close to the airport, which was a plus. It was also one of the first singles apartment complexes in the nation and there was a party most every night. It was sometimes so rowdy that the neighbors would call the police.

There were four women assigned to our two bedroom apartment on the second floor. It was new and clean with a small living room and kitchen and two bathrooms. My roommate was from Seattle, I remember. We had men passing through the apartment all hours of the day and night until I finally said no more, no one could come there after a certain hour of the night. I was the one who organized the food and cooking, in the interest of saving money, which the others weren't really interested in.

This was where I met my first husband, Warren. There was a party going on one evening after classes, well every evening, in fact, and I wandered down and into this one apartment on the first floor. I met this guy and talked with him for a while. I can't even remember his name, but he was a friend of Warren's and still is to this day. He was really good looking and interesting to talk with. But for some reason he walked me over to where Warren was and introduced me. It was Warren who then pursued me, asked me out to dinner and we started dating. Warren had a new white Corvette, and it was fun riding around with him. He said he lived in this big house on Minnehaha Parkway; I found out later, when he took me to meet his parents, that it was his parent's home and his mother had bought him the Corvette. He said he was divorced, but I found out later that the divorce was not final. He was a graduate from the University of Minnesota. He had a good job with the bank; he was already a manager in his twenties. So I overlooked the little lies and thought this guy was going to be very successful. The message to me from my mother was to find a man who could support me in the style to which I was accustomed, whatever that was. He was good looking as well and looks were important. Now when I think about it, those were terrible values to be teaching a daughter. But I have to take some responsibility as well, I went along with it. I didn't think about whether he was a loving, caring and compassionate person or he would be a good father. But this was what I was taught and you have to remember, I was still escaping.

I graduated from stewardess school and I had a choice of bases, Seattle or Washington DC. I chose DC thinking about my new relationship and that I could get back to Minneapolis sooner.

I packed my blue Samsonite luggage my grandparents had given me for high school graduation, with all of my worldly belongings, and boarded a flight for Washington DC. I was twenty-one, alone, knew no one, and didn't have a place to stay when I got there. I told the crew that I was "dead heading", that's what they called it, to my new base, and they said to stick with them and they would help me. I, in fact rode most of the way in the cockpit and I remember coming into National, the old DC airport, flying over the Potomac River and the capitol, seeing the Washington Monument all lit up that night. It was magical; I was enthralled.

After we landed—I think it was a DC-7, jets were not on line yet—the crew caught a cab and we were taken to the Willard Hotel, where we would be staying. I found out later that this was the hotel of presidents, very historic and very old.

The next morning I put on my uniform and went to the airport with the crew. I already had a schedule. I was to fly every day—yes, that's seven days a week—from DC National to Detroit, with stops in Pittsburg and Cleveland. We had a four hour layover in Detroit, for which they provided a hotel room at the airport hotel. Then we would head back to DC arriving in the early evening.

I left my luggage in the crew lounge and went to find my flight. I had no idea where I would be going when I returned that night. But I could always go back to the hotel if I had to.

When I boarded the flight, an old DC-6 the workhorse of the skies in those days, I met the other stewardess that I would be flying with. She asked if I had a place to stay and I said no. She offered to have me stay in her apartment in Alexandria that she shared with another woman, and I immediately accepted.

We came back that evening, flying in between the thunderheads of a late day thunder storm. Then we took a cab to my new friend's apartment. As it turned out, I would be sleeping on the couch in the living room with an airline blanket and pillow. But I didn't mind. Hopefully, I would be going back to Minneapolis in a couple of months. And we were seldom in the apartment: flying every day and out on the town every evening. DC is a party town. I don't know how I had the stamina, but I did.

Later in the second month, Warren drove down to see me and my mother rode along. I took off the next weekend and we ditched Mother and drove to New York City. I had never been there before, and I was dazzled by the skyscrapers and the glitz. We went to the Johnny Carson show and then out to dinner. After dinner we went to the top of the Empire State Building, the tallest building at the time. We talked about marriage, but Warren didn't exactly propose. He wasn't a person who made commitments and also, technically he was still married, which I didn't know.

Chapter Twelve

The appraisal came back under the selling price, the buyer started negotiating and we had to drop the price. We had expected this. We all finally came to an agreement as to what the price should be and who would be responsible for various repairs and we were good to go. The closing would be in late December. I was glad this was almost over. Now I could take care of the bills and put this all behind me.

I continued sorting through the artifacts, finding wills and bank books dating back to the early thirties. There were also photo albums. One with black and white photos that looked like they were taken before the turn of the century. The women were dressed in ankle length dresses with large hats and high button shoes and the men in suits of that era. I had no idea who these people were. What was I going to do with these? Maybe donate them to some historical society. I didn't know. I hated to just throw them out, but I didn't want to keep them either.

One photo album did have photos taken when Alan was young and Grandpa was with us. Birthday pictures, Christmas. I would keep these.

I found my mother's high school diploma and booklets from

Hamlin University with the rosters of students and saw both my mother's name and my father's. I remember my mother telling me how, when she attended college, my grandparents would not pay for her to stay in the dormitory, so she had to ride the streetcar every morning to get to school. She lived on Abbott Ave South not far from Lake Harriet, west of what is now highway 35 and had to travel across town to St. Paul where the university was located, probably about ten miles. No wonder she couldn't keep up with her studies; that was a long, slow ride on the streetcar. And cold in the winter time. Thinking about this now, it seems that her parents set her up for failure. So she did the best she could and then found someone to marry, and escaped. But she escaped into what turned out to be a loveless marriage of drudgery, and then she wanted to escape again and that was what she did.

I came back to Minneapolis from Washington DC early that fall and got a one bedroom apartment near the airport. Actually Mother found it for me and wanted to move in with me, and I said no to that. I was finally free, I thought and I didn't want Mother monitoring my every move.

I had more seniority now and better schedules. One was flying to Seattle, laying over a day, then on to Miami, stopping in Chicago. And then back to Seattle by way of Chicago and the next day taking the red eye back to Minneapolis. I was gone for seven days and then off for three. It was wonderful. On one trip I skied at Snoqualmie pass and then a day later I was sun bathing on Miami Beach.

Mother was still meddling in my life. She would call me before a flight to tell me that she loved me and wanted to talk with me before I left in case my plane crashed. I don't think she really said that, but I thought at the time the inference was there.

Somehow she and Robert got a key to my apartment from the

BATTLE OF THE WILLS

superintendent, and she found out that Warren was sleeping there. I was livid. Still hadn't escaped. Yet.

Mother went to California to live; San Bernardino was where her friend Sam lived. Robert soon would follow. He was driving out about the middle of December, and he asked me to go along. I had a few days off, so I said yes. We took my cat along as well; Geisha Girl, my first Siamese. I had gotten her soon after I came back to Minneapolis, wanting to have a pet. I also had a bird that I had in college. I thought that cats were more flexible than dogs; you could leave them alone for a couple of days with food and water and a sandbox. If I was gone more than two days, Warren would help care of her. Well, the problem was when I came home from a trip, Geisha Girl had her sights on the parakeet, and I knew the bird was not long for life if I left Geisha alone with it, so I gave the bird to a friend.

Anyway, we drove out in Robert's new, baby blue Ford convertible. I had brought my cat with me, We traveled south to New Mexico going over the Raton Pass then continued south, trying to escape the storms that were blowing through to the north. Outside of Las Vegas New Mexico, the storm caught us, and we were stranded for six hours, with driving snow drifting on the highway. We were stranded, along with about thirty other cars. Geisha Girl did fine, but I was worried the top of Robert's car would blow off and expose us to the elements. It didn't, and the plows finally came through. We were able to move out of there and spent the night in Las Vegas.

After visiting with Mother for a couple of days, I flew home, with Geisha in a carrier in the cabin of the airplane. The storms diverted the flight to Denver and I had to stay overnight there with the cat, but I eventually got back home. And Robert was now back with Mother, where he wanted to be.

Later that December, I had not had my last period and I was

very tired. I went to a doctor in Seattle to confirm what I already thought; I was pregnant. I started to have morning sickness on my flights. When I told Warren, he said that we had better plan the wedding. His parents supported the idea; they liked me, and I think they wanted him off their hands. He needed a wife. He was good at business, but domestically challenged. By that time his divorce had become final so that obstacle was gone.

We were married in the Little Brown Church in the Vale in Nashua, Iowa on February 17, 1962. That's the church mentioned in the song that was so popular in the forties and fifties, Church in the Wildwood. The wedding party consisted of a few friends, Warren's parents, my mother and brother. We all drove through a blizzard that fateful day to get to the church in time for the wedding. I remember dressing in the church basement and then walking through the snow to get to the ceremony in the chapel and my matron of honor, Linda, my roommate my freshman year, dropping the groom's wedding band in the snow. We searched for an hour and never found it, and so the minister lent us his wedding band for the ceremony.

We stayed in a dumpy motel on our wedding night with a photo of Niagara Falls over the bed. The next day we drove the Corvette through the raging snow storm with drifts as high as the car and more than once almost went off the road. A Corvette is one of the worse cars you can have for driving in those conditions. A day later, the storm let up and when we got to Springfield, Illinois, I bought him another wedding band. Though he never wore it all the time we were married. I guess that was a flag right there.

Not long ago I looked at the photos of our wedding. Mother cried, and looked very sad. Maybe she was getting back at me for crying at her wedding. But she was not supportive of the marriage. To be expected. I didn't tell her that I was pregnant, but she probably suspected. Getting pregnant before the wedding was frowned upon in those days. Robert gave me away as I didn't have a father. He had a sad look on his face as well, but that was normal for him.

We honeymooned in Key West Florida, driving all the way in Warren's Corvette. What a trip. The car was so uncomfortable, and I was not feeling well anyway in the second month of my pregnancy. After Key West, we drove up the west coast of Florida, and then around the Gulf through Mobile and on to New Orleans. It was just before Mardi Gras, and the streets were already packed with revelers. I remember we stayed in an historic bed and breakfast in the French Quarter. The food was wonderful, what I could enjoy of it, and musicians roamed the streets playing ragtime and Cajun music.

One day we boarded a local bus to go down to the wharf. The bus was crowded, but I saw an empty seat towards the back of the bus and went back and sat down. The black woman next to me turned her face as I sat next to her. I didn't think too much of it until after I got off the bus and Warren yelled at me for sitting next to this lady. I just looked at him and asked why. I didn't understand. He told me that because we were in the south we couldn't sit next to Negros. I didn't know and I didn't believe that. I was from the north, and we didn't think like that in the north. I was taught that we were all equal.

After we got home, I was never so glad to be out of that car. Soon after, Warren decided to sell it as it was not a family car; where would we put the baby?

The next month I was ravaged with morning sickness so much so that I became dehydrated and had to be hospitalized. But during the fourth month when I began to show, I started feeling better. We moved into a two bedroom basement apartment in Bloomington where Warren had an agreement for us (me) to take care of the complex in exchange for a smaller amount of rent. I say me, because he was never there to do it. I was to vacuum the hallways, shovel the walkways, make sure the grass and flowers were watered in the summer.

On September eighth I went into labor, and Warren took me to the hospital. It was a long labor as first babies usually are. Warren sat with me for a time; he'd brought a wooden gun stock that he was refinishing—he was a gun collector. At about six a.m. the next morning our baby boy was born. We named him Alan Warren. He was only five and a half pounds but was healthy, and the doctor said he was not a preemie. It was the happiest day of my life, holding this child in my arms; he was beautiful, and I vowed that I would be the best mother I could for him.

We brought him home to the apartment, and I had not lost all of the fat from being pregnant. I remember Warren telling me that if I got fat, he would divorce me. I worked really hard over the next few years to prevent that from happening, but not necessarily for Warren's benefit. In fact, when we moved to California when Alan was three, I weighed only 100 pounds, pretty skinny for my 5'5" frame.

Another event stands out in my mind during those first days at home with Alan. My brother-in-law, Marsha's husband, would stop by the apartment periodically to just chat for a while. I didn't think anything of it. He didn't put any moves on me then. But when Alan was a toddler, Marsha asked if I would go out to their home and watch her kids while she had some surgery. She had three boys at the time. Tory was four or five and the twins were six or seven months I think. It was summer and there were tornado warnings every night, so I was lugging three kids into the basement along with the new puppy they had. Bruce came home from work that first night, he was in construction of some type, and after dinner he started to hug and kiss me, and I pulled away and said no, this can't happen. I then called Warren and told him he had to come out to Bruce and Marsha's house and stay at night, and he did. What a fiasco that would have been if I had an affair with Bruce while Marsha was in the hospital. I never told Marsha about it. She later separated from him, but they never divorced.

The next couple of years were difficult for me. In fact, the remaining years of my marriage to Warren were not happy times. But I was determined to stay with it. I didn't believe in divorce—at that point. For better, for worse. We moved from the apartment to a small house in Golden Valley in West Minneapolis, and I was happy to be living in our little home.

Warren left the bank. I should say here that Warren's father, Dudley was a Vice President at the First National Bank in Minneapolis, and no doubt that helped to promote Warren into the position he had there. But Warren worked hard. He took a job with Gold Bond Stamps, located not far from our home in Golden Valley, as IT manager, and he traveled—a lot. He was seldom home. And when he was in town, he came home late at night and sometimes not at all. He didn't think he owed me a phone call. I just became used to it and lived in my own world with taking care of Alan and our little home. I bought a cocker spaniel, and we named him Sammy after my mother's friend, who we later called Uncle Sam.

Somehow I got pregnant again. I guess I say that because of Warren's long absences. Of course in hindsight, what was I thinking? But I didn't know what a loving marriage should be like, so I accepted my circumstances and tried to compensate. And I wanted two children. I didn't want Alan to grow up as an only child. I delivered another beautiful baby boy on the 21st of February that next year. We named him Randel. I brought him home from the hospital and several days later noticed that he wasn't eating like he should and was losing weight, which shouldn't be happening.

I called the pediatrician, and she told me to bring him in to see her. At her office, she examined him and then immediately called for an ambulance, and they took Randel to the hospital. Warren and I followed in the car. For several hours we waited, pacing the corridor of the hospital, and finally the doctor came out and said she couldn't save him and would we like to go into the operating room and say goodbye. Words can't describe how I felt at that moment. He was a beautiful, healthy baby when he was born. He weighed more than Alan had. My grief was inconsolable.

Mother had come to visit to help me with the new baby, and when we got home, we told her the horrific news. I went into the bedroom in seclusion and cried and cried until no more tears would come. My mother-in-law, Muriel, called to find out how the baby was, and she immediately went into action. She came to our home to comfort me and gave me some tranquilizers; they didn't help. Then she helped by planning the funeral for baby Randel, and I was thankful to have her do that. I was stricken with grief and couldn't think or make decisions. He is buried in the Lakeside Cemetery in Minneapolis, and when I was back in Minnesota a few years ago, I visited the gravesite with my baby son.

Let me say something here about Muriel, my mother-in-law. She was, yes she's gone now, the most loving, caring person but also the most meddling. I remember when we were first married, and Warren was having a birthday, she wanted to bake the cake for him. I said no, I was his wife now, and I wanted to do that. When we moved into our first home, she wanted to decorate. Warren was the little prince in the household when he was growing up; the favorite—he had two younger sisters. She actually spoiled him so badly that it has affected his whole life, and he suffers because of it today. But when I was married to Warren, I never said an unkind word to her. I had disdain for her, but I would never have been disrespectful to her.

BATTLE of the WILLS

Warren's parents are in fact another story. His father Dudley Mays was from a fairly prominent family in Utah. His grandfather was a senator, the first non-Mormon, and his uncle was a Judge. Muriel's family was even more interesting. She grew up in Corsicana Texas. Her father was a wildcatter and part of a team that brought in the first oil well in Texas. This was the start of Texaco oil. They went from rags to riches so to speak in a very short time. And they spent the money, buying a large home and a Packard car, the Rolls Royce of the 30's. Muriel attended SMU, and she probably majored in music as she was an accomplished pianist. Alan told me once that he'd heard Muriel had had an abortion when she was a teen. Of course that's hearsay.

I am not sure how Muriel and Dudley met—maybe at college. But this was the era of the flappers and they, even in those days, consumed a lot of alcohol. And later in life they were addicted. I didn't realize this when I first knew them, although the alcohol flowed freely when I went to dinner at their home. But then I drank a lot in those days as well. I always quit alcohol when I was pregnant, though as I knew it was not good for the baby.

When Warren was a teen, they lived in a home in Bloomington that had a guest house out back and Warren was allowed to live in that house with no restrictions and wasn't required to be at family meals, if there were any, or participate in the family in any way. Of course these were the habits that he carried on throughout his life. He was never a family man. He supported us, but that was the extent of it.

A couple of months after Randel's death, we found out, or the doctors did, what had caused him to die. As it turned out, Warren and I had a blood incompatibility; my blood was/is B negative and Warren's O positive. This seldom affects the first born baby. If they had known, which they didn't, they could have exchanged Randel's blood after he was born, and he would have lived. Evidently my obstetrician or the lab where my blood was tested, made an error. We talked about a law suit, but I wasn't up for that. And it wouldn't bring our baby back any way. Randel was gone.

So I tried to have another baby. I had asked my obstetrician if he thought I could carry a child to term, and he said that I should try. I know, what was I thinking? I was still mourning the loss of Randel. And why would I want to have another child with a husband who was never there, was not a loving person to me or Alan? But I didn't know any better. I had grown up in a dysfunctional family as well and thought this was the way it should be. Again, I didn't want Alan to be an only child. I did want them to be closer in age than Robert and I were, thinking they would be better friends if that were true. And if I became pregnant now, they would be about three years apart, which was perfect.

Chapter Thirteen

The house in Redlands is sold and closed. I received a photo book of the house from Rita, and I loved it, but I cried as well. The end of another time in my life and the lives of Robert and my mother. Now someone else will be living there and making memories with a family, and I hope they are happy. My family was seldom happy; there was always so much turmoil.

My living room is now cleared. I took more things to the thrift shop, and I did throw away some as well, but most of this memorabilia is in a couple of boxes that I put in my shed. I still have the two little chairs, and I think I am going to have to part with them as well, because I have no place for them in my home. But again, I hope someone will buy them and enjoy them as our family did for so many years. I have all of the paintings hung on my walls, and they are beautiful. The enhanced photo of Yosemite is hanging in my bedroom and the little watercolor of lupine is in the TV room. Those two pictures were sitting on the floor in my mother's bedroom. The statue of the three graces, which I gave to my mother and she never displayed, is sitting on my chest of drawers in my bedroom. There are other mementos now throughout my house, like the little ceramic birds that Mother collected. I didn't know Mother had such a love for birds. I love these things as well, and I will cherish them. But I wonder who will have them when I am gone.

After I became pregnant with my third child, I was in my eighth month and I didn't feel any movement of the baby. From experience I knew, that is a very active time for the fetus. I thought then that the baby might be dead. The doctor said to wait a week or so but then called me in and said I would be taken into the hospital and they would induce labor.

I was awake, I remember when the baby came out and there was a murmur from the doctors. My pediatrician was there as well, prepared to exchange the blood if the baby had been alive. But he wasn't. Yes, it was another boy.

After delivery of the stillborn child I was taken to another floor for the two days where I would be hospitalized as they wanted to have me away from the maternity floor where everyone had babies; I didn't have one anymore. I was numb with grief again.

I came home to take care of Alan. I went into a deep depression for I think about a year. It's kind of fuzzy to me now. I didn't want to get up in the morning, I didn't want to get dressed, I couldn't concentrate to read, couldn't drive a car. Life had no meaning for me, except that I had to take care of Alan. I had no one to help me either. Warren was MIA as usual. Muriel worked so she wasn't there to help me. My mother was in California. I was so alone. But then I reached out to a minister. I don't even remember his name. He said that I should get out of the house and do some volunteer work to get my mind off the tragedy in my life. And that saved me.

Maybe a year or so after this happened, Warren said that we should move to California and we talked about it, and I agreed that would be a good thing to do. I think we were both tired of fighting the cold winters and the summers weren't so great either with high humidity and mosquitos. I thought too, it would give a fresh start to my life and maybe our marriage. He interviewed and got the job with Fairchild Semiconductor located in Mountain View California. I remember when he went for the second interview, I was invited along. His boss took us for dinner, along with his wife. I'll never forget as we were waiting for our drinks, his boss started playing footsie with me. At first I just thought he was putting his feet in the wrong place, or maybe my feet were in the wrong place, but then when I moved my feet out of the way, he moved his feet over to mine. I never said anything to Warren. I didn't want to jeopardize Warren getting the job. I wanted to move to California, and I didn't think I would have to deal with this guy again.

Also, as Warren was negotiating the job, I told Mother that we were moving to Northern California. Well, it just so happened that my grandparents by this time had left Northfield, Minnesota and lived in San Jose. Perfect. It would be wonderful living near them. But Mother was not happy about this. She wanted me to come to Southern California so that I could be closer to her. I would have thought that she'd been happy for me to be close to Grandma and Grandpa, but she wasn't. Of course I would go where Warren's job was.

My grandparents are amazing people in that they had a pioneering spirit and that is likely where I get my strength. They were in their mid-seventies when they decided to sell everything and move from Northfield, Minnesota to San Jose, California. They had tired of the winters and neither Robert nor I were going to school in Northfield any longer—they no reason to stay. After selling all of their furniture that they'd had for years, some bought as newlyweds, they packed their car with only the essentials; my grandfather's tools and my grandmother's sewing machine and of course their clothing. They didn't have a destination. They drove their 1952 mercury to Los Angeles, and then worked their way up the coast to San Jose, looking at the different cities trying to decide if they wanted to live there. I can just imagine what Grandma thought as she was riding along on a ten lane freeway out of LA. It must have been terrifying for her, especially since she never learned how to drive. When they reached San Jose, they decided that was the place but, living in a motel, it took them a year before they finally bought a house. They told us laughingly they had worn out the cars of a couple of realtors. California agreed with them. They were gardeners, grew beautiful roses and other flowers, and they were reasonably happy for another ten years.

We moved into a really nice home in the Westgate area of San Jose. I loved it. It was sunny and warm. The neighbors were friendly. The school was around the corner, and I started getting involved, working in the school library and volunteering. We found a wonderful Congregational church with a minister who had a down to earth message for living a meaningful life. I counseled with him several times about my marriage. I joined a women's church group. I was coming out of my depression and becoming present in my life, but it had taken a long time.

    We had brought our cocker spaniel, Sammy, and our Siamese, Geisha girl, with us. Unfortunately, Sammy got out one day; he was not neutered and was looking for a female to mate with and was killed by a car. We waited awhile, and then bought a black cocker spaniel puppy and named him Robbie.

    Another weird incident, though in San Jose. My neighbor came over to introduce herself soon after we moved in and we became good friends, having coffee in the morning, joining a bowling league, and we even started to hang out with them as a couple. Her name was Jean (not her real name) and her husband's name was Ron (not his real name). Well, not too long after we lived there,

BATTLE OF THE WILLS

her husband started to come over to visit in the afternoon; he was a salesman for a drug company, and he had flexible work hours. I didn't think too much of it at first. We had been out to dinner with Ron and Jean, and I considered both of them to be friends. But after a few months of this, when he came to visit me he started trying to kiss me and make out with me and said he wanted to go to bed with me. And I thought, oh no, not again. Even though my marriage was not the best, I wasn't up for an affair. I kept putting him off, and he finally gave up. I wondered, what was it with me, do I have a look of being vulnerable, a target, that men think they can approach me like that? But I think he was another one of those men who just liked to play around with anyone who was willing. I think Jean knew he was doing this. But we never talked about it.

Three years later, Warren took another job with Singer Friden. They had a new large computer division, and he was awarded the MIS position, Management Information Systems. The job was in Oakland California and that meant he had a ninety mile one way commute every day. We bought a little Honda Civic that had terrific gas mileage. But after a year of this we decided that we should move to the Oakland area. We found this beautiful home on a hill overlooking the valley and Mt. Diablo in Dublin, California, a small town about twenty-five miles east of Oakland. We said goodbye to our San Jose friends and packed up our furniture and other belongings and moved. I remember we even packed the cat; she was missing for a time and we found that she had slipped into one of the boxes. Fortunately we were able to rescue her.

Dublin was like living in the country. We were surrounded by ranches, and I could hear the cows mooing at night if I had my windows open. There were fields of poppies in the valley and lots of critters around as well: skunks, rabbits and raccoons. I think there was a nest of skunks under our house, as some mornings we would awaken to skunk odor, and one evening our dog, Robbie, chased a skunk in the back yard while we stood by the patio door watching not knowing what to do. The dog came running to the door and when we opened it to let him in the house, the skunk nearly came into the house as well.

Dublin was a great place to raise children. The school was at the bottom of our hill and within walking distance. At the top of the hill was open land for miles, a wonderful place for kids to explore.

Dublin was a true awakening for me. Again I got involved with volunteering at Alan's school. I joined the garden club, and in fact was the head of the annual fund raiser one year. I need to point out here that people who lived in Northern California at the time were very socialistic and supportive of one another. Unfortunately that is not true in Arizona.

I started to paint in oils and showed my work; a couple of paintings were sold. Alan became a Cub Scout and I was the den mother, and I loved doing that. We had friends and neighbors who got together for wonderful parties. At the suggestion of Joy, the wife of Warren's boss and a friend, I learned how to play tennis. I had a happiness that I hadn't had in years.

We also were trying to adopt a child. We had started the process in San Jose, and then when we moved to Dublin, I contacted the Children's Home Society in Oakland to try to bring another child into our home. I had thought maybe an older child, a boy of three or four that would be closer in age to Alan, who was eight years old at that time. We had started the screening process, but it was short lived. When I told Mother we were adopting, she told me that she would not accept an adopted child as her grandchild. But then she hadn't really accepted Alan either, she said because I became pregnant before I was married.

Singer Friden decided to divest their large computer division, and that meant Warren's job was going away. It also meant that we would move again, and of course I was heartbroken. But, since we were dependent on Warren's job to support us, there was little choice. I was captive.

Warren interviewed in Southern California, and we looked at homes in some of the more affluent areas like Palos Verdes, Santa Monica. Some of them had maid's quarters in the garage; how could people treat their help that way? We were invited to dinner with one of the men from the company, who would hire Warren, and his wife—I don't remember their names. They took us to their "club". I guess they were trying to impress us. I wasn't impressed. I wore a mini-skirt, and the wife gave me looks like I was out of place. But then I kind of marched to my own drum beat in those days. I was probably the first woman to wear a bikini at the Westchester Country Club pool in upstate New York when we visited one of Warren's relatives several years ago. And I had the figure to do it.

I didn't like the idea of moving to Los Angeles. Then Warren got an offer from Diamond's department stores in Phoenix, Arizona. He took the job. Diamond's had been locally owned by the Diamond family but had been bought out by the Dayton Hudson company in Minneapolis. And Dayton's, another family owned department store was well known to me; this was where we shopped from the time I was a little girl.

I had been through Phoenix several years before with Robert on the trip to California, and I didn't think I would like Phoenix. At that time it was winter, a cloudy day, dreary and brown. I was used to green from Minnesota and California too. Again, I didn't have a choice. I was only along for the ride.

Warren took the job, and we decided that he would work for a few months while I stayed in California during that time. I was happy with that decision as I wasn't anxious to leave Dublin and my friends. It was Thanksgiving by the time I went to Arizona to look for a house. When I arrived, I saw a different Arizona than I had seen before. Maybe I wanted to see it in a better light, but I loved the mountains in the middle of town, and the desert was lush and beautiful, full of vegetation, flowers and cactus. There was plenty of room to hike and bike and be outdoors, and that was my and Alan's lifestyle. This might be an okay place to live except for the heat in the summer. But this was November and it was paradise. Within a week, I selected a 2400 sq. ft. four bedroom home in Paradise Valley, consisting of two and one half baths, living room, dining room, family room with a beehive fireplace and a lovely kitchen. The house had an acre and a half of land and wonderful views all around. There were five horses in a paddock next door. I loved it and was ready to move.

I went back to Dublin to pack up our belongings. We put the house on the market, and it sold quickly. I remember so well the last couple of nights in the Dublin home. There were cartons everywhere waiting for the moving van; it was kind of eerie. That last night, I went for a walk up the hill overlooking the valley and I cried. It was dark and cold with the clouds hanging low and threatening to snow, which seldom happened here. I didn't want to leave behind the friends and the life that I had made here. And what lay ahead? I didn't know. Could I have the same happiness in Phoenix? I didn't know, but I would try. I was an outgoing person and made friends easily. One very sad note; we couldn't go forward with the adoption since we were moving, and we had just been approved and were ready to select a child. I was heartbroken about that. But maybe we could adopt in Arizona.

Chapter Fourteen

During the time that we were moving to California, Mother and Robert were living together. She had gotten job as an administrative assistant with the Board of Realtors in San Bernardino, and later she went to work in Palm Springs for about a year. Robert was, I believe, working for an insurance company. I had been in contact with Roy by phone. I think he called me asking about her. I had such a high regard for him as he was so kind to me when Mother was married to him. I guess I just wanted to maintain the friendship.

I remember going to visit Mother. I had told her that a couple of times I had talked with Roy. But this night when I talked about it, she went ballistic. She said all I wanted was to get money from him, which was so far from the truth. I cried which seems to be my behavior when I am attacked like this, and I left the apartment and went for a walk. It was late at night, and I was fortunate that I wasn't raped or killed. I think now, as I look back that she didn't come up with this on her own; Robert was feeding her these ideas. But she believed them and went with it.

Over time Roy kept calling me and asking about her. So I finally said, "Why don't you call her and find out for yourself." And he did. Eventually he came to California to visit her. As it turned out he had missed her terribly. After Mother left Roy, his sister moved in with him in Waseca and they weren't getting along at all, so I guess he asked her to move out and he was alone. Like most men of that era, he didn't do well being alone.

One thing led to another. And they decided to remarry; this time with a valid prenup I would guess. I wasn't in on that. I was happy for her. She wasn't good on her own either.

Then came the tug and pull with Robert. Mother didn't want to leave Robert, but she had to go and live with Roy in Waseca when they married. And of course she didn't want to leave sunny California either, and I can't blame her for that. Roy had a little apartment and eventually Mother talked him into buying a townhouse on the lake, which he didn't want to do at first. But I had visited her in Minnesota and saw the apartment and it was dreary. Roy certainly could afford something better.

I visited them after they bought the townhouse on the lake and it was lovely, except for the mosquitoes. I recall sitting out on the deck looking out on the lake. The sun was setting and I heard this buzz above my head and looked up and saw a hoard of mosquitoes. As the sun went down the mosquitoes descended as well, I have a little painting that I did while I was there of the farmland behind their home. It was a peaceful, bucolic place to live; other than the bugs. But that was Minnesota.

About this time Robert had bought a little home in San Bernardino. I think he paid $21,000 for it. He planted flowers and fixed it up, which increased the value. And so for the next couple of years, Mother and Roy would spend summers in Minnesota and winters in California in Robert's home. It was a good solution, I thought.

In the meantime, Grandma developed colon cancer to which she succumbed. Grandpa told Robert after she died that he was happier now that she was gone. I guess she was probably bitching at him most of the time. Then at some point a couple of years later I think, Roy had a heart attack in Waseca and died alone in their townhouse on the lake. His daughter, who lived in town found him. Mother told me that she called her and just blurted out on the phone "Daddy's dead". Probably upset that Mother wasn't with him to take care of him. I don't know.

So now Mother had no conflict between her son and her husband. She could look out after Robert and not feel guilty about not being with Roy. Then things started to unravel. Robert was shot while driving around in a bad area of town. The story was that he had stopped for a red light and some guy came up to his car and shot him through the window. The bullet passed through his shoulder, traveled across his chest, but fortunately missed his heart or any other vital organ. He survived. I went over to see him when he was in the hospital. I don't recall if Robert was working during this time or not. He seemed to frequently jump from one job to another.

Sometime in this period Robert started hearing voices. He was also threatening suicide. Of course, Mother was beside herself with worry. She called me for advice, which she seldom did. Most of what was happening, she kept to herself; I guess she didn't trust me or maybe she was embarrassed; I'm not sure. She told me about Robert being in trouble and what was happening with him and asked me what I thought should be done. And so I just said if he's threatening to kill himself, you need to get help for him. Seemed pretty simple and straightforward.

Mother kept calling me and telling me that he refused to get the help he needed, and she was fearful that he would carry through with his threats to take his life. She said that the only way she could get him to the hospital was to call in the police and have him committed to the psychiatric ward of the VA hospital, and she asked me if I thought she should do that. I told her that if that was the only way he would go, that was what she should do. And Robert was taken forcibly to the hospital.

They could only keep him for two weeks with orders from his physician. During this time, they evaluated him and determined he was paranoid schizophrenic, and they prescribed some medication for him. I went to visit him in the hospital, and he was very subdued. He was released a short time later.

I am not sure of the sequence of events after this. I think he probably had trouble finding steady employment. Mother said he refused to take his medication. But then if the pills made him feel lethargic and inadequate, I could understand. But the alternative was having the voices and dealing with his own demons.

Sometime in here, he sold his little house. I think Mother said that he came away with some seventy thousand dollars in cash. And then he disappeared for about a year. Mother had no idea where he was; he never called her to let her know that he was okay. She didn't know if he was dead or alive. Well, she was so upset, understandably. She kept calling me and telling me about it. I didn't have an answer for her. There was nothing she could do but wait until he would decide that he was either coming back or letting her know what was happening to him. Was he punishing her for intervention? Possibly. I think now, and didn't think of this at the time, but Mother likely told him that it was my idea to send him to the hospital. I don't know this for sure, but it seems like this is what she would do to take the blame off herself. And of course that just exacerbated his hatred for me. Oh, the tangled web. There were no winners in this family.

In the meantime, Mother had inheritance by now from Grandpa, who had passed away a couple of years earlier, and from Roy, and she had social security so she didn't have to go out and get a job, which was good. But she was living in these dumpy apartment complexes where she was fearful of intruders harming her and her car was being vandalized in the parking lot. And then she found this home in Redlands on Finch Avenue. She called me to come over and look at it. And I did. She was unsure as to whether she should buy it; they were asking $92,500 for it. A lot of money in the early eighties.

She was living in a small apartment at the time in Redlands and having to rent a garage a half a mile away, walking back and forth every time she wanted to go somewhere. And she said a couple of times men were following her. Well, this was not good.

We went to look at the patio home. This is the three bedroom house I describe earlier that I just sold as part of the estate. There was also a pool and a tennis court, which I doubt neither Mother nor Robert ever used. I remember looking at the orange grove across the street and wonderful views of the mountains to the east. I said buy it. Absolutely. And she did.

One observation here, is that while Robert was away, Mother depended on me much more than she ever had before. And she seemed to trust my judgement. I'm sure that was because I was the only one available at that time. She had no one else. When Robert was with her he was her go-to person. I have learned in my long life that I am the only person I can really trust and the gives me a strength to work through any tough problem that might occur. It took a long time to realize this. And I also have learned to love myself because if you don't love yourself, you can't love other people.

Not long after she moved into her new home, she heard from Robert, and boom—he was back at her place with a car full of dirty clothes, she told me. No explanation as to where he'd been. But she, of course, took him in, no questions asked. I wasn't surprised. But I had my life to deal with and I didn't dwell on this. What I realized later though, was that this was the time when Robert was facing his sexual orientation. It had to have been traumatic for him, especially since gays were not accepted in the 80's; they still aren't today by certain segments of our society and in different areas of the country, the ultra-conservative South East for instance. I wasn't bothered by this news; I accept people on the basis of their integrity not on the color of their skin or the people they choose to love. Robert was still my brother, and I would try to love him if I could. And my mother too.

Robert had a place to live now. He paid no rent, but to be fair, he designed and planted lovely flowers on the patio, decorated the kitchen with yellow floral wallpaper and helped with the cleaning and upkeep. He needed a safe haven as he was often out of work, and I was glad that he had it. Plus, Mother needed him. She couldn't handle things by herself.

Before Mother died, he was doing some appraisal work, and he did buy a rental home but didn't keep it very long. I'd heard that he couldn't get along with any of the tenants; he was hovering over them all the time making sure they took care of the place. You can't do that with tenants. There is an unwritten law of quiet possession, whereas the landlord needs to allow tenants to live in the rental home undisturbed. I don't think he understood that concept.

But in general, Robert didn't get along with very many people. And it was good that he had the place to live with Mother and that she had him to help her. They depended on one another like an old married couple.

To be fair, however, I was as dependent as they were. I was a housewife for sixteen years. I had fewer job skills than Mother had. But I was raising a child, and I felt that that was my first obligation. When Alan was grown, I could do more or less what I wanted. So I stayed in a loveless marriage. I had found a way to be reasonably happy by finding meaningful activities and surrounding myself with friends. I thought I could do this forever and let Warren support me in the style that I was used to. So I went about my life working at trying to be a good parent, got involved in volunteering and playing tennis, and gardening and many other activities. But that was all about to end.

Chapter Fifteen

We drove across that desert in December of 1973 to our new home and life in Arizona. Christmas was a week or so away, and I had bought a small artificial Christmas tree so we could have a small celebration of the holiday. As I was watching the desert with the cactus and unusual plants, I thought, Jesus was born in the desert. Those who have researched and studied this, however, think Jesus wasn't born in December but in July when the census was taking place. The holiday was hijacked from the pagan's celebration of Yule and celebration of lights in the dark time of the year.

So we settled into our new home and Alan began school at Kiva, a K through 8 school. I remember taking him that first day. I walked with him to his first class, and we opened the door and the classroom was filled to capacity, maybe thirty students in a very small room. That worried me. But the alternative was Judson School, a private grade school, and we weren't prepared to do that. In those first months, I kept in contact with his teacher and monitored what was happening.

Alan took the bus every day. The school was not that far away, but too far to walk. The bus stopped on the street over from our house, and I would meet him and we'd walk past the horse pasture to our house. Often we'd play table tennis while we talked about how his day went. The teacher said Alan was advanced enough to go into a special class for gifted children, and I was pleased about that because then the class size would be smaller.

    I on the other hand was quite lonely. Alan was making friends at school, Warren had his colleagues at work and ham radio friends, but I wasn't making much headway with new friends in the neighborhood. There were only six houses on the block and no one seemed very friendly. An attorney lived across the street and he had polo ponies, while a German couple resided next door, and I didn't get to know the rest of the people. One woman two houses to the east who was about my age, and I don't remember her name, finally wanted to be friends two years later when she needed someone to watch her house while she and her husband were on vacation.

    So I decided that I would have to reach out to meet people. I joined a tennis league and met some really nice friends that way. I joined the Phoenix Art Museum and became a docent, studying art history for two years so that I could give tours of the museum and go out and give talks in the community. I continued to volunteer at Alan's school. I was room mother, helping to plan field trips, providing treats for the various holidays, like Valentine's Day.

    I played tennis almost every day. I started running, two miles at first and then worked up to five and ran some ten k's and eventually, later on, started running marathons. I also started going on ski trips. I had done some day trips to ski areas when we lived in Dublin with a girlfriend that I knew there. I loved skiing, and I wanted to do more of it so I joined Phoenix Ski Club. Well, I didn't know it then, but this ski club had a reputation.

    I remember walking into my first ski club meeting. I wore black boots and a short skirt and sweater and I was noticed. The men

BATTLE OF THE WILLS

were looking me over. This group was known for being a great meet and greet group, many were single, and what I found out later married or not, they liked to have fun. I went on my first ski trip and had a wonderful time. We skied all day and went out to the local bars and danced all night.

What I didn't realize, or maybe I did, was that I was pulling further away from my marriage. We had little in common. His work took most of his time, and I helped with entertaining, giving parties for his people and having his boss and wife for dinner occasionally as I had always done. But Warren's free time was spent with his ham radios or shooting; he was a big gun collector. I hated guns, and I wasn't interested in ham radio.

When we first arrived in Arizona, I thought again about adopting and had looked into it, but it occurred to me number one, I basically had no help in raising Alan and I wouldn't with another child either, and number two, it was obvious that the marriage would be ending and it wouldn't be wise to bring a child into a broken family. And then with Mother saying she wouldn't accept our adopted child, I would have no support. And so, sadly, I had to let go of that idea. I think the good news here is that I was finally facing reality.

During Alan's younger years, Warren had little or no involvement with raising him, and I was okay with that. I actually didn't want Alan to spend much time with his father as I realized early on that Warren was not a good role model for him. And then the burden was on me to raise Alan; I was much like a single parent for those early years of Alan's life. Warren did support us however and that was certainly a help.

I hadn't wanted to work outside the home as I always felt that someone needed to be home with the children. I remembered those early teen years in my life where I had little supervision and I got into trouble. Warren, however wanted me to go back to work.

His mother had worked as long as I had known her. She really didn't have to, as Warrens' father made plenty of money, he was a bank vice president, but Muriel had expensive tastes. So to appease Warren I took a day job with a credit bureau when Alan was about six months old and took Alan to day care. After two weeks got sick and I quit my job but then found a hostess job in a nightclub where I could be home with him during the day and I had hoped Warren would be with him at night. But Warren never came home so I had I had to find a sitter.

Now we seldom had sitters when Alan was little. We maybe went out to dinner once a year, on our anniversary. Never went to movies or the theater. I don't think Warren wanted to spend the money. When there were McDonalds, though we did take Alan with us and he splurged for some hamburgers and fries. But I was used to this behavior so I didn't complain. My parents were much the same; they seldom went out in the evening and I can think of only one time when we had a baby sitter when I was little.

The hostess job was terrible; my boss had me wear an outfit like the playboy bunnies wore and I resisted and showed up in a demure cocktail dress and told him I wouldn't wear anything else. Again I had men leering at me as they came into the club. And I had to drive 30 miles every night and came home at 2 a.m. Even my own mother was unhappy about that. But I got pregnant and soon quit that job never to work again until I took the clerking job at the department store when I was considering a divorce. Now, I have to say here that I think it is important for women to have a career of their own even when they are married. Marriages don't last, a spouse can expire. And just for her own self-fulfillment. But again, I say someone needs to be watching the children.

Then in Arizona, Alan joined Boy Scouts and I could no longer be involved. It was all about the dads, and I was happy about that, but a little sad too, because I missed my Cub Scouts.

BATTLE OF THE WILLS

The Scottsdale chapter he joined was big on hiking. They went on hikes about once a month, which wasn't Warren's forte, but I have to give Warren credit, he tried to participate. They took this rafting trip down the Colorado River. I think they rafted from Havasu City to Parker or something like that, not in the canyon. I felt left out and was a little bit jealous. So I found my own river trip; rafting the Grand Canyon in oar boats.

We were a small group of people, about twelve of us, some from ski club. We began our adventure by hiking down the Kaibab Trail on the South Rim into the canyon and getting on the Zodiac type rafts at Phantom Ranch. It was a split trip, and the people who had rafted this far hiked out of the canyon. I remember the cost was $250, outrageously inexpensive compared to today. We rafted 120 miles of the canyon in seven days. It was the trip of my life to that point. We pulled the Zodiacs onto a beach every night when we could find one. One night before we reached Lava Falls, we were in the narrows of the canyon and there were no places to pull off. We were on the river until 10 p.m. that night and some of us were concerned. I wasn't one of those; I thought it was so beautiful with the full moon shining into the canyon creating eerie shadows on the canyon walls. And it was quiet and peaceful. Few people see the canyon this way.

We hiked side canyons, finding Indian ruins and secret little grottos with rushing waterfalls at Elves Chasm.

Our food was cooked over a campfire, and we slept on the ground out in the open with no tents, and I remember waking in the morning to see the sun rising on the canyon walls and also seeing a rainbow that formed over the canyon one afternoon after a storm. We hiked about 9 miles from the river to Havasu Falls, and seeing the travertine falls for the first time was amazing. In the next couple of years I would hike to this falls from Hualapai Hilltop two more times.

There was not a lot of wildlife to be seen although we did see desert big horn sheep, which are much smaller than bighorn sheep I had seen when I was younger in Glacier National Park. One day when we were searching for a campsite, we came upon a nest of rattlers with babies coming out of small crevices everywhere. Needless to say we didn't camp there.

Overall it wasn't a dangerous trip, although one raft flipped in Crystal Rapid and everyone swam the rest of the way. And then we came to Lava Falls, the biggest rapid on the river. I have to mention here that I am not good in water. I am not a proficient swimmer. I think it partly goes back to when I was a child. Mother was always fearful that I would drown for some reason, and whenever we were near a lake or a river she would say, "Don't go near the water. You'll fall in and drown."

I carry that with me to this day.

But Lava Falls is terrifying. This is a big rapid, a 5 on the scale—6 being the highest—at mile 171 on the river. People have died in this part of the river. We climbed up on a ledge and stopped to scope it out before we rafted it as was usual with the bigger rapids. Then we got into the rafts and started sliding into the rapid, hitting the chute, our guide attempting to keep us out of the upcoming holes. The raft was tossed about. Then we went completely under the water, and I thought we were goners, but we came back up and hit the wall across the canyon and we were out. Exhilarating. I felt more alive than I had ever felt. Especially since we all survived.

Later that night after dinner, I went down by the river alone and took off my clothes and stood there feeling the air around my body, looking up at the full moon. I was alive. And I was going to live the life that I was destined to live. Not with this loveless marriage that I was a part of. There had to be something better for me, and I would find it. I washed with some soap and took a dip in the river and then dried myself off. I was a new and different person.

We took out at Peach Springs, pulled the rafts out of the water and deflated them so they could be carried to the waiting trucks. Seven days with no news of the world. Was it still there? What had happened while we were gone?

They bussed us back to Flagstaff where our cars had been parked near a motel. And I slowly drove home to Phoenix and the life I so much wanted to change. But it wasn't time yet. Alan wasn't old enough. I had to wait a little longer.

I remember coming home that night and not wanting to sleep in my bed. I had been sleeping out in the open for a week and I liked that, so it was difficult going back to sleeping in a soft bed confined by a roof instead of seeing the stars overhead.

Warren and I kept growing apart, and it would be a matter of time before we would be divorcing. I knew this for a couple of reasons. When we lived in Dublin, I believe he had an affair with his secretary. Her name was Sharon, and when he came home at all, that was all he talked about; Sharon this and Sharon that. The gossip at the office was that they had some kind of a thing going on between them. And I saw evidence of another indiscretion when he was living in Phoenix while I was still living in Dublin. The marriage was broken and had been for a long time. We hadn't been sleeping together for a long time and there was little or no communication between us. The only opportunity for us to talk was when we were riding together in the car and Warren made sure that wouldn't happen. He had a mobile ham unit and was constantly talking with his ham buddies and tuning me out.

Then there was a money issue. He had started putting me on a budget. He had a separate account that I didn't have access to, and then gave me a household account of $120 a month to run the household; pay utilities and buy food. There was no money left for me to buy clothes or other things that we needed. I think he was hoping I would get a job, but I wanted to be at home. Alan was going into his teen years and to me it was even more important for a parent to be at home during those years. I complained, but he was in charge. On the other hand, he was spending freely on guns and ham equipment while we were living like paupers. I had always been very frugal, sometimes making my own clothes, always saving money on everything. As I mentioned earlier we seldom went out to dinner. It was, I guess, the last straw so to speak. I felt like an underpaid maid: cleaning the house, cooking for him, washing his clothes, taking his suits to the dry cleaner. And that's what I was.

I wanted out of the marriage, but I was frightened. I had no work skills and I was apprehensive to throw myself out there and maybe live in poverty. What I did do at this time was get a job so that I would have some kind of a resume when this all finally came about.

There was another complication. Alan was a young teen. And he was caught up in the drug culture of those days. I had found a bong in his bedroom and showed it to Warren telling him that our son was using drugs. Warren refused to believe it. For whatever reason, he wasn't going to help. Either he didn't care or just wasn't willing to get involved; I don't know. But that was typical. It was all on me to do the parenting.

Over the next couple of years, it was a battle. There was the time when Alan had a friend stay overnight with him. He was such a polite, nice young boy. And then in the morning, the neighbor in back of us knocked on our door and told us that he found Alan and this young friend packaging marijuana, obviously intending to sell it. Now you might admire their entrepreneurial spirit, but what they were intending to do was illegal and they could be sent to prison. The man said that he would give us a chance to call the police and if we didn't, he would. I called Warren, who was at work and told him about this. He didn't know what to do, and I couldn't turn my son into the police. But the neighbor did, and the Paradise Valley Police came out and took Alan and his friend into custody. They must have been all of 14 years old. They took them into the Paradise Valley Police station and booked them, finger printed them, had mug shots taken. Now when I say Paradise Valley Police Station, this is not your usual police station. Paradise Valley Arizona is extremely affluent, and it no more had the feeling of a police station than the school office. Warren and I went to get him, and the officers talked with us and recognized we were concerned parents and they wouldn't press charges—this time. But if it happened again? I think they were trying their best to scare the you-know-what out of these boys. And it did. But over the next couple of years there were more incidences, including an overdose episode which frightened me more than anything.

Parenting is the most difficult job there is. Especially in our complex world, with so many hazards and temptations. It is also the most important job. I was dedicated to raising Alan to be a caring, loving person and a successful and happy adult. I made mistakes, but there were times when I was so worried that he would be sucked into the drug culture and never get out. I think I may have been too worried. He eventually took charge of his own life, which was the goal, and he is doing well.

Chapter Sixteen

So I went skiing at Vail Colorado. And it changed my life forever. The first night we were there, I was at a party with ski club in the lobby of our hotel. As I was standing there holding a glass of wine, this man with dark curly hair and big brown eyes came up to me, introduced himself and said, "I would like to take you to dinner". I was taken by surprise, but I looked at him and said, "You can take me to dinner, but I'm not going to bed with you."

The next night we went to dinner. He told me he was from Atlanta, Georgia and he was a doctor. I don't remember what else we talked about during dinner, but I do know that I looked into those big brown eyes and I was hooked. After dinner he went to his room and brought a guitar to the lobby and we sat on the floor in front of the fire, while he played and sang to me. Then we started kissing, and one thing led to another. We went upstairs, he kicked out his roommate and we had sex and spent the rest of the night together.

The next morning, when I started thinking about what happened, I was amazed at what I had done. I didn't even know this man. Was he telling me the truth? Was he really a doctor from Atlanta?

We spent the rest of the week skiing and sleeping together when we could find the privacy. A couple of evenings he joined our group for dinner and some parties. Then it was time to go home. He came with me to our bus to see me off, and I remember watching him out the back window of the bus standing there waving to me. And I thought, well I'll never hear from him again. But we had fun.

The day after I arrived home, I was in the kitchen, Warren was standing next to me and the phone rang and it was Michael, the doctor from Atlanta wanting to know when he could see me again. I was blown away. When Warren asked who had called, I told him the truth.

Warren moved out within the week to a singles apartment complex in Phoenix and not long after that *he* filed for divorce. Now, I could have just said it was a ski friend on the phone and not told him, but I think I was ready for the separation and the divorce. It was long overdue. I would have done it much earlier had I not had the death of the babies and the depression and if I had had a means of supporting myself.

Michael visited me in Arizona for a week and we drove around the state and went up to Carefree and stayed at a motel there. Then he invited me to come to Atlanta and we spent the next two weeks hiking, making love, traveling around the state, making love. I hadn't realized how starved I was for someone to really love me. And Michael loved me. He treated me like a queen. He was thoughtful, and generous and kind. Everything that was missing from my marriage.

We went to Savanah, had dinner with a friend of his who he had gone to med school with. His friend had a shrimp boat and we went onto his boat, picked up a bucket of fresh shrimp and went back to his modest little home where he and his girlfriend lived.

BATTLE OF THE WILLS

We smoked a few joints, cooked and ate shrimp until we could eat no more and laughed until our sides hurt. I remember on the way back to our hotel, passing out shrimp to the bell boy in the lobby.

We went to Jekyll Island for a couple of days and swam nude in the ocean. Then drove up to the mountains and hiked, climbing the first leg of the Appalachian Trail in the Smokey Mountains of Georgia.

I met his ex-wife, and he had his young daughter come over and stay with us in his home when we were there. She was a delightful little girl. It began to look like this was a serious relationship that I wasn't ready for. I had just gotten out of a marriage. Did I want to go and live in Atlanta? Michael was ten years younger than me, but that shouldn't be a factor.

I came home to the reality that I was divorced and Alan had gone to live with his father. I was devastated when that happened, but I understood it. It was time for him to spend more time with his dad now. Alan was only fifteen when the divorce happened, the same age as I was when my parents divorced. But I missed him terribly, and every time I saw a blond boy about his age, I thought about Alan.

I remember moving out of the big house in Paradise Valley. The house was empty and I sat down on the step of the sunken living room and cried, thinking of all the birthday parties, Christmas celebrations we'd had here. And what was before me was unknown. Could I survive? Could I support myself? I didn't know. I knew I wasn't ready to jump into another marriage. I had to get to know myself better before I became part of a couple.

I had rented a cheap two bedroom apartment down on Indian School and tenth street, not a bad part of town but not ritzy either. I moved in with my two cats, and Warren and Alan took Robbie our cocker spaniel. As I was bringing the last of my things into the apartment and it was late, maybe ten o'clock or so, I noticed this guy tippy toeing around the complex in shorts. I didn't think too much about it. But when I finally had everything in the apartment and had closed the door, there was a knock on the door. I pulled the curtain aside and looked out the window and there he was—jerking off against my door. Thank goodness I was smart enough to not open the door without looking first. I yelled at him in my meanest voice, "Get out of here, I'm calling the police." And then I went back into the kitchen and cowered for a few minutes, scared to death. I am thinking, what am I doing here? Maybe I made a mistake in divorcing. Too late now. I was committed. Problem was, I didn't have a phone yet, but he didn't know that.

During this time, I was working at the department store selling scarves. They had made me manager of that department, because I was selling a lot of scarves. The scarf counter was on the way to other areas of the store, and people often stopped to look at the displays that I had on the counter. When they stopped, I would look at their clothing and pull out a scarf that I thought would go well with their outfit, and most times they would buy it and another one as well. Suggestive selling I called it.

At night I was hanging out with friends at meet and greet bars and clubs. We'd have a few drinks, usually the men buying and then we'd go to the Jockey Club and dance. Never met anyone this way, and I always went home alone. But it was kind of fun. Phoenix in the early 80's was one big party, every night of the week.

One night I went home to the apartment and I as was getting ready for bed, I heard some scuffling on the balcony above me and a woman cried out "Who are you?" She was being raped. I called the police; I don't know if they got there in time. I was shaking. I decided that I would have to get out of this apartment complex and find a safer place, maybe a house. Even though I had a lease, I wrote the manager a long letter telling her what I heard that night and that I didn't feel safe. After that, when I was out in the evening,

BATTLE OF THE WILLS

I always had a friend come with me back to my apartment and walk me to my door.

When I divorced, I had laid down some rules; I couldn't get pregnant, or raped, or get a DUI, or have an auto accident. I understood that those kinds of events could destabilize my life and send me spiraling downward, and I wasn't about to let that happen. I was on the edge as it was, but I was on my way up.

So I had the realtor who sold our big house in Paradise Valley search for a house for me. After looking at several and making an offer on one and losing that one, I finally found my house on Wagon Wheel. I offered the full price, about $43,000. I had received $20,000, my half of the equity of the PV home, and I put ten thousand down and the rest in the bank as back-up money for emergencies. The lender was skeptical of giving me the loan; it was unusual for single women to buy houses in those days. And to make matters worse Warren went off to California and didn't pay off the department store bill along with some other bills that we had while we were married, leaving me to start my single life with bad credit. What a guy. But I wrote a letter saying that I was a good risk. I still own that house today; free and clear. Smartest thing I ever did.

I remember the day I moved in. It was Thanksgiving weekend, 1978. Renting a U-Haul truck, I had asked a couple of friends to help move the small amount of furniture from the apartment to my house. That first night in my new home, I felt safe and secure.

I also wanted to have a house for Alan to come to when he came back, and I knew he would. I wrote to him often. I sent cookies. I sent warm clothes. And in a year's time Alan and Warren came to Arizona, and Warren said that he was sending Alan back to live with me. It seems that things weren't going well with Alan in California, for whatever reason. I was really happy.

I prepared a room for him in my home. At first he went back

to his old high school in Paradise Valley. He had a motorcycle his dad had bought him. But it was quite a distance for him to go every day, and so we decided that he would go to Central High, closer to our home in Phoenix. My home was in one of the best school districts in Phoenix; that was one reason why I chose it.

I don't recall how long Alan lasted at Central, but not very long. To be fair, he was in his senior year and coming into a new school is tough. I did it in my junior year, but that was a small homogenous community. Phoenix has diversity, and gangs; it would be difficult for anyone.

Not long after he started there, Alan came home one afternoon and said that he was quitting school. I was not prepared for this. But he was 18, and he could decide on his own. Now, his father said when Alan came back to me that he would pay child support, all of $125 a month for Alan if he was in school. So now that money went away. And I was hoping Alan would go to college, although his dad said he would not pay for it: no surprise there.

I was working, but a clerk in a department store doesn't pay very much. Warren was paying me some alimony for the next five years, when he thought about it; I often didn't received the money. So I said to Alan that if he wasn't going to school, he had to get a job. I didn't want him hanging around the house smoking dope and drinking beer.

And the drugs and alcohol were another issue. How would I deal with that? I decided to defuse it instead of fighting it. So Alan and I sat down one evening and smoked a joint together. Then I told him he could have alcohol at home but not when he was driving. He was almost an adult. The drinking age was/is 21 in Arizona, and so we were breaking the law. I don't know if this was effective—likely not, as he continued to use drugs and alcohol, and as I said earlier, overdosed one time.

Alan got a job at the hotel a quarter mile from our house so

BATTLE OF THE WILLS

he could walk to and from work. He started as a dishwasher and worked his way up into the kitchen as prep cook and then chef. He decided that cooking wasn't going to be his career, so he found a position as the audio visual technician for the hotel. And that was the beginning of his career as a sound engineer: the work he is doing today.

I am extremely proud of him and how he has managed his life and pulled himself together. He got his GED, went back to school and received his associate's degree from Phoenix College. He worked for a cable company in Phoenix for a time but then went to Los Angeles to work. I thought when he left, that he was all grown up and I wouldn't have to worry about him any longer. He was in charge of his life. But a mother is always a mother, and I will always worry about him and want the best for him.

After Los Angeles, he applied and got a job with George Lucas Films as a sound engineer working at Skywalker Ranch in Northern California, and he worked for them for 15 years. Then he struck out on his own and is freelancing for companies like Apple Computer, LinkedIn and doing very well. He bought a home in Petaluma a few years ago and he has married.

Chapter Seventeen

I ran my first marathon the year I was first divorced. I trained every weekend, running 10 to 15 miles at a time. I never did the 20 miler that is a requirement for being successful in running the marathon. And some of my friends said I wasn't trained well enough, one of them a male ski buddie, whom I skied and played with.

So I went out there that morning in December, and it was cold. We wore plastic bags that we could discard as we started to warm up while we were running. I started out slow and kept a steady pace, and I was feeling great at the ten mile mark. I came up on Tex Earnhardt—he owns a bunch of car dealerships in the valley—and ran with him for a while. Then a few miles later, I saw my ski friend, who said I shouldn't run, beside the road, totally spent, and I laughed at him as I jogged by. Cruel I guess. I finished with a four ten, four hours and ten minutes. Pretty good for not training properly. I chided him the next time I saw him at ski club meeting. He was a jock, very athletic and washed out of the race.

A couple of years later, I ran the Heart of San Diego with Jon, I think after we were married, and I didn't finish; I crashed at the 20 mile mark. An ambulance picked me up and when they checked my vitals they said I was in better shape than they were. They took me to the finish line which was in a football stadium and I was ashamed to get out of the ambulance; I didn't want any friends seeing me coming in an ambulance. That was in the spring. In the fall of that year I ran another Fiesta Bowl marathon and had my best time ever; 3 hours and 38 minutes.

But I want to warn every one of what not to do after running a marathon. Don't go car shopping. Don't do it. I did, and I came home with a new Honda Civic, an impulse buy, because I was so high on endorphins after the run. I needed the car though so I guess it wasn't really an impulse buy. I had received the Ford Torino from the divorce, with front wheel drive, a big engine and it was hell on ice for driving to the ski areas.

I thought about the year before when I had taken Alan skiing to Telluride and I was driving the Torino. The day we left to drive home, it started snowing, big flakes drifting down. I didn't even have chains, forever the optimist, but I was able to borrow a pair from a guy I had met up on the mountain the day before. We put the chains on the car that morning and then started up the mountain. There were other cars on the road, and I should have followed behind them, but no I was a trail blazer. I passed them all and forged ahead. As we climbed higher, the snow was coming down faster and thicker, until when we reached the summit of Lizard Head Pass, at 10,000 feet and it was a whiteout—I could not see where the road was. I asked Alan to roll down the window and stick his head out to try and see the road. Then quite suddenly we slipped off the road into the ditch. Alan turned to me and said, "Now what?" At first I was somewhat alarmed, but then I told Alan that we would be okay. We had plenty of fuel, food to eat and clothes to keep us warm, we were on a main road and someone would come by and pull us out. I got out of the car and stood in the road trying to flag a car down to help us out. I must have looked like a wild woman in my rabbit jacket with long hair flying in the wind. Several cars honked as they passed by. Then a truck came lumbering up the road and stopped. I went over to ask the driver if he would pull us out, and to my relief he said yes. It was a supply truck for a movie they were making in Telluride. After they pulled us from the ditch, I asked if I could follow him down the mountain, and he said that would be okay. No more trailblazing. We carefully wended our way down the mountain on the icy road with rocks sliding from the banks alongside the road.

Once we were off the mountain, the road was clear and dry all the way across the reservation and on into Flagstaff. But it wasn't over yet. When we reached Flagstaff, there was a big dark cloud hanging over the town and as we drove south on I-17 it rained liked it had never rained before. We came into Phoenix, and I wanted to keep going south to Glendale Avenue and take Lincoln Drive across, but Alan talked me into turning off on Bell Road. We came to the underpass, and it was flooded and there were several cars waiting to go through. I stopped and surveyed the situation and asked if I could drive through and one of the men said, "Go right ahead and gun it."

"If I get stranded will you push me out?"

And they said yes. I was naïve; I didn't know when you drive fast through high water, the carburetor gets wet and the car will stall, but I do now. Which is exactly what happened. We stalled in the middle of the flooded underpass and the water came spilling into our car. I rolled down the window and yelled "Help" and someone with a truck came and pushed me out and on up to a nearby gas station where he pulled out the carburetor, dried it off and we were on our way. I think those guys had a big laugh over this dinghy woman getting stranded in the underpass. We arrived home in Paradise Valley about 7 o'clock, after being seventeen hours on the road.

The little Honda Civic hatchback that I bought would be much easier to drive on icy roads and had great gas mileage. Although I did go off the road a couple more times and the car was white and it got lost in the snow bank a few times.

So I had a new car and a house payment and then I lost my job. I had gotten this little receptionist job with one of the large law firms downtown. It was such a boring job that I had a hard time staying awake, especially since I was out partying every night. One day I must have nodded off and a client reported me. A couple of weeks later when I asked for some time off; they fired me. It was no loss; I hated the job, watching the male attorneys abuse their secretaries.

What to do, go skiing. Michael had invited me to spend a week in Aspen with him. I flew Denver to meet him there. While I was there Marsha, Warren's sister, met me at the airport for coffee. Marsha and Bruce had moved there a few years earlier from Minneapolis. She was now separated from her husband—you know the one who was hitting on me a few years back? —but she never really divorced him. She lived out her life in a mobile home and died several years ago. I think she had a sad life.

Michael met me in Denver and we caught a flight to Aspen the next day. I hadn't seen him in months, but it was like we had never been apart. He had been in New York for a time but was back in Atlanta starting a new computer imaging company for medical procedures.

That morning we had to wait for the flight to Aspen as the weather had socked in, but we were finally able to board this old DC 3 no less. They are a very reliable work horse however. But flying into Aspen is a little tricky, coming over the mountains and then the pilot has to immediately drop down to the runway, something like my barnstormer when I was flying a few years ago. We landed safely, as I knew we would.

BATTLE of the WILLS

We skied hard, made love a lot, and ate a lot. Then the last day we were there, I said that we should take off on our own for the day. Michael was okay with that. I went out to the mountain and put on my skis and took the lift to Aspen Mountain, which had more black diamonds and expert runs. I was coming down the mountain and encountered a small group of guys skiing the bumps and having a great time. Somehow I got in the middle of them and we started racing to the bottom. I skied with them for a couple more runs and found out that they were all members of a Canadian Hockey team. Well, that was exciting. Then I left them and got on the lift again. It started to snow, and I had left my goggles behind in the room. What was I going to do? I was lamenting to the fellow riding the lift with me. "No problem," he said. "I'll buy a pair for you at the lodge at the top of the mountain." "Okay, but I Will pay you back." Although I didn't have enough money with me.

Well, he bought the goggles for me, and then invited me to his condo. Yes, he owned a condo at Aspen. So I accepted. Yes, I was a risk taker. I have to say I would not do that today. We went to his condo and had some wine. He said he was in manufacturing and had flown up to Aspen in his jet. Well, I thought that was pretty interesting. We talked for a couple of hours; yes that's all we did.

"I would like to visit you in Phoenix," he said.

"That would be okay." I gave him my phone number thinking I would never hear from him.

I didn't tell Michael about my afternoon, except for the Canadian Hockey team, which he thought was very funny.

Several months later I had a phone call from the guy I had met in Aspen. He had just flown into the Scottsdale airport and could I come and get him. I drove to the airport, picked him up and took him to the resort hotel near my home. We agreed to meet for dinner later in the afternoon. When I went back to get him for dinner, he started right in making moves for sex, and I thought this man didn't come to see me, he came here for the sex. But then why was I surprised? Then he became surly, and we didn't go to dinner after all. He said he was leaving in the morning and I said fine. He said he thought I was more of a hippy type and here I had a house and a conventional car, and wasn't the fee spirit he thought I was. I guess he expected me to be driving a Volkswagen bus and living in a commune. But even with all of his money, I wasn't attracted to him. No great loss.

Upon returning from Aspen, I had to face the fact that I had lost my job. And I had payments. So what to do? Look for work, and then I asked Mother for the first and only time for some help, and she gave $300 to tide me over. I never had to ask her again, thankfully.

Those next couple of years were filled with anxiety of finding work that would pay enough to support me. I took a job with Motorola running parts for the various projects. This was government work, building parts for missiles and bombs, and I had to have special clearance which was no problem. However, when I found out exactly what we were making in that manufacturing plant in Scottsdale, I was not happy, and I guess I said some words to that effect. And then I couldn't keep up with the work. I had several projects that I was responsible for, schlepping parts in 100 degree plus heat across the parking lots.

One of the Mechanical Engineers was trying to date me, but I wasn't interested. And then I was fired from that job.

But I had a friend who worked for this WABCO repair shop in south Phoenix. I told him that I was out of work. He got me an interview and I was hired. The job entailed preparing estimates for wheel motors of the huge mining vehicles. The office was located in south Phoenix. I went to work at 7 a.m. and often had to step over winos languishing on the doorstep of the building.

The office was over the repair shop, and I had to go down onto the floor and get information from the mechanics in order to write up the estimate. That entailed learning all of the parts of these huge wheel motors and how they worked. I had to wear working blues, steel toed shoes and a hard hat when I was in the repair area. Needless to say, I learned a lot about wheel motors and mining, and I enjoyed the challenge, but I was the only woman in the shop, and the boss was like a pit bull, sitting in an adjacent room with a picture window watching the office workers, me and another man. But it was more money than secretarial work paid. And I never fell asleep.

I think I was laid off from this job as well. Or I quit. I don't remember which. Then I met Jon, my second husband. We started dating, and I moved into his house near Paradise Valley Mall. Alan was still living with me, but I was going to have to rent out the house so he would have to go and live with his father, who had moved to Scottsdale by this time with his new wife.

While living with Jon, I wasn't working, so I became a Mary Kay Consultant, which Jon always belittled. Granted, I didn't make any money, but I will say I learned perseverance and how to set goals, and these are things that have I carried with me for the rest of my life. I didn't sell that many cosmetics, but the consultant that brought me into the program was a fashion model, and she did informal modeling in the finer restaurants in Scottsdale. I said that I would like to do that, and she arranged for that to happen. And that was how I started a small modeling agency. I found more restaurants and shops that wanted to show their clothing, and I had more work than I could handle, so I trained and contracted other attractive women to work with me. These were middle aged women who lived in Scottsdale. I recruited and trained them and they worked for me on a contract basis. We were fairly successful. We showed the clothing during lunch. Many times our audience would go to the shop and buy what they had seen and they sometimes would buy right there in the restaurant. We started to get mall shows, some print work and even a TV commercial. I was having fun and making some money too. Jon never shared his paycheck with me. I was still expected to be self-supporting and contribute to the household.

In the beginning of our relationship, we seemed very compatible. We ran together, marathons and 10Ks and hiked and backpacked in Arizona and Colorado. We went to Durango and took the Durango to Silverton Train and got off at Needleton, which was about the halfway point, and then hiked about six miles into Chicago Basin and made camp. I will never forget walking up the trail the next day and the profusion of flowers of every different color. We climbed Mt Eolus, a fourteener, but it was in the afternoon and a thunderstorm rolled in, which was an everyday occurrence in the summer in the mountains. I remember how we ran for our lives to get down below the tree line so that we wouldn't be hit by lightning.

Another time we were coming back from a Colorado backpacking trip and we decided to take a side trip and hike the north rim of the Grand Canyon. It was August, the weather was warm. We started hiking down the trail—our goal was to hike to Roaring Springs. When we were several miles into the canyon, it started to rain and we decided to turn around and hike back up to the top of the rim. It wasn't raining hard, but waterfalls appeared where there had been none before and rocks started flying from above. One flew by Jon's head and almost took him out. We heard a rumbling, tumbling sound, and I asked Jon, "What is that?" "Hug the wall," he said as a huge boulder came crashing down in front of us. I have never hiked so fast in my life as I did that day to get out of that canyon.

I have to tell the story about the time we hiked into Superstition

BATTLE OF THE WILLS

Mountains to camp overnight. It was the middle of summer, monsoon season in Arizona and it had been raining the last couple days. I remember standing in front of Jon's house looking up at the clouds and we looked each other and said, no, it won't rain tonight. That afternoon we hiked into the area at First Water, back to Gold Canyon where there was a small creek running through. We unpacked and started a camp fire for dinner, and then soon after dinner settled into our sleeping bags for the night. The rain started with big drops and then became a small deluge. We pulled our ground covers over us, we didn't have a tent, thinking that if we could keep dry we would be okay but water was running all around us. One of us got up and looked at the creek and it was rising fast. It was time to move to higher ground. We took our sleeping bags and walked up a little hill and that was where we spent a very wet night. Had we stayed in our camping area we likely could have been washed away.

Then we started going to Telluride and hiked and backpacked in that area as well. We also skied in Colorado and Arizona, downhill and cross country and had many other adventures. It seemed to be a match made in heaven.

After a couple of years, Jon and I married. Before we married, Jon was insistent we would have a prenuptial, and I couldn't understand why; neither of us had much money and it didn't look like we were going to be making a lot of money in the future. I thought prenups were just for people with a lot of money. We each had houses with mortgages and not much more. So it looked to me like he wanted to preserve his future earnings—really his because he didn't share—that he made for his children, yet he was doling out thousands for them, buying a new Jetta for his youngest daughter for high school graduation, paying for wedding trips and much more.

So we went ahead with the marriage, I think at my insistence, because if we were going to be couple I wanted to be married in spite of all the warning signs. We had a lovely wedding in the Desert Botanical Garden in Phoenix at sundown on the 24th of June, 1985, with about thirty friends attending. My son gave me away—well that was tradition, and Jon's three daughters were there, his youngest with a pouty look on her face the whole time. I didn't invite Mother or Robert. Two days later we went to Grand Cayman for a little honeymoon. But it wouldn't last

After we married, he wanted a post nuptial. And there were other problems. He had three daughters, and two of those daughters really hated me, because I guess they thought I had taken their dad away from them and they treated me badly. They were young teens at the time, and the two oldest daughters had already had to deal with a stepmother. It was complicated. I understand this now. And some of their behavior had to do with Jon's history and background; that's a book in itself. He came from a dysfunctional family as I had. But he was a loving person, and I thought when I met him that we could overcome anything if we loved one another.

After five years of turmoil and some issues that don't even matter anymore, I decided I didn't want to be in another marriage where there was no partnership. He was partnered with his daughters, which I guess he had to be for a time, but it looked to be never ending. So we split.

I have to say that when I married Jon, Mother was not happy. One indication was that when I sent photos of the wedding to her, she sent them back to me. Did she see the problems before I did? But I loved Jon and thought we could make it work. Well, we couldn't, and I didn't want to fight through it.

So we filed for divorce, an amicable divorce; after all we had never comingled anything. No joint bank accounts, we each had a house. We took the minimal possessions that each of us had and went our separate ways. But before we did that we had a divorce trip.

I was still living in Jon's house because my tenants hadn't moved out yet. We were having brunch one Sunday at one of the resorts in Scottsdale, and Jon invited me to go to Hawaii with him. I think he felt guilty, because he had sent two of his daughters to Hawaii for their wedding trips; I thought the groom was supposed to pay for the wedding trip.

We went and I loved Hawaii but there was a lot of tension, and it wasn't the trip that we would have had if we had been looking to our future together.

When we came home and the divorce was final, the recession hit. My modeling business was all but gone; the stores weren't buying my advertising services. I was divorced again and out there without a job. Fortunately one of my clients, an owner of a golf and tennis shop, hired me as assistant manager and buyer of women's clothes. I accepted and that was a help for a while.

I moved back into my little house on Wagon Wheel, and I was never so happy to be home again. I should never have left. I had Willy, my Doberman that I had gotten before I met Jon. She helped to make me feel safe.

But I was sad too, and Christmas was coming up, and I was alone. I thought about going somewhere for the holiday, and when I searched the internet, I found a company that was offering cross country skiing trips on the north rim of the Grand Canyon. Perfect. I signed up and invited Alan and then Jon—yes we were still friends—to join me. Alan invited his step-sister Amy, who was about his age, to come along.

Two days before Christmas we drove north on I-17 to Flagstaff and continued north on highway 89, turning off at Marble Canyon on 89A. For some reason we stayed overnight near there and then drove on to Jacob Lake the next morning, Christmas Eve. At Jacob

Lake we boarded a snow cat that would take us the thirty miles to the lodge near the north rim of the canyon. The road to the north rim is always closed in the winter, October through May, as they have an abundance of snow in that area. It was like a fairy land with snow on the branches of the juniper and pine trees. When we reached the lodge and were signed in, we were taken to our yurt where we would be staying. What is a yurt, you might want to know? It is basically a hexagon shaped tent structure that is used by the nomads in Mongolia. It was fairly large and had a small wood box stove on one end. There were bunk beds and the yurt would hold ten or so, although we had this one just for our group.

After skiing a couple of hours in the afternoon, we went to Christmas dinner in the lodge. It was so beautiful. With a fire burning in the large fireplace and a huge Christmas tree with lights and decorations sparkling in the firelight, we could feel the holiday spirit. There must have been about twenty people from all over the country. The buffet dinner with turkey and all the trimmings was delicious.

Then we went back to our yurt. It was ten below zero that night and for all of the other nights we stayed there. Although we plenty of wood, someone had to get up in the middle of the night to keep the fire going. That was Jon for the most part. He was a good sport.

The next day we skied out to the rim of the canyon. Words can't describe the beauty with snow all around and on the ledges of the descending canyon walls. We gathered some wood and built a small fire and cooked soup.

One more night of freezing nighttime temperatures. But it was so magical to be there. The yurt had a small round window in the middle of the ceiling and I remember looking up that night and seeing the stars sparkling through the window frosted with icicles.

At noon the next day, we were to return by snow cat to Jacob's

Lake and then home. They loaded twelve of us onto a new snow cat that the fellow who was running these trips had just bought. Evidently this was the maiden "voyage" for the vehicle and this guy got carried away and really gunned up several little hills until finally we heard the gnashing of gears and we stopped. He got out and evaluated damage and then came back and told us we were going to be there for a while. We were stranded, fifteen miles from both the lodge and Jacob's Lake. We didn't have radio communication. And it was ten below zero. Some of us tried to stay warm in the snow cat for a time, but the gasoline fumes were so bad that they could not remain there.

I and some others looked at our situation. It was about 3 p.m., and it could be hours before anyone came to get us. We had warm clothing, we even had food that some had brought along on the trip. We all gathered pieces of wood in the area—there was a lot of it—and stacked it together and built a huge bonfire. With all of us standing around the fire to keep warm, we exchanged stories of our lives and our adventures. It was a special moment I think for everyone. We soon forgot that we were stranded in the snow in ten below weather fifteen or twenty miles from civilization. Many hours later, it was nearing 10 p.m., we saw the headlights of another snow cat coming down the trail. It was a much smaller vehicle, and they could only take 3 or 4 of us at a time, and it was near 2 a.m. before we were all back at Jacob's Lake. Then we had the long drive home. Jon stepped up again, and said he would drive. That was a Christmas I will never forget.

I was making all of 10 dollars and hour at the pro shop, and I said to Jon that I couldn't make it on that amount of money, pay my bills and save for retirement. I had no benefits, no pension of any kind. So he said, "Why don't you learn computers."

"I hate computers."

And then Jon said that the PC, personal computer was coming on line, and it wasn't like main frame computing. And he thought I was smart and could learn how to program.

So I gave it a try. I bought a $3,000 PC, a box and a monitor. I bought a book on programming database SQL, Sequel Query Language, bringing data to the windows application. I studied every day and night, learning how to program with a 4GL language to design windows apps for business applications.

After three years, there was a job at the county. Jon was working as a consultant with this company, and they put me into this job in December. I had to tell my boss at the pro shop that I was leaving; it was the holidays and he wasn't happy, but I told him that I had to take care of myself.

I was 53 years old when I started my first job in computing at the county and it was white knuckle time the first few weeks. But I did have some knowledge of database design and distributed apps and the engineers only knew main frame. So I designed and created a small windows application, and I was on my way.

From there I went to work for Intel for a year and then Charles Schwab for two years. I was making decent money and had health insurance and was maxing out my 401K for my retirement. Life was good.

Needless to say, I wasn't doing a lot of skiing or playing tennis, but I was supporting myself and saving money. I wasn't dating that much either, not really interested in meeting anyone to be truthful. One of the analysts at Intel asked me out, and I dated him for a while, just going out to dinner occasionally. He always complained about paying the bill when he took me out, and then during the election when GWB was running, he said he was voting for Bush. Well we got into a shouting match. I said that Bush would be starting wars; I don't know how I knew that. Anyway, that was the end of that relationship.

BATTLE OF THE WILLS

I decided to go to Oregon and work. I traveled to Portland and interviewed with PGE for a programming position. I was hired. I went home and put my house up for sale and then went back to Portland and bought a house. But just as all of this was happening, Mother died.

I came back from Portland after working a week with the contractor whose job I would be doing, and I was not feeling good about anything. The contractor who was training me was sending strange signals, I think he was angry about losing this job, and I was dependent on him to train me. And with Mother dying, although it was a blessing as she had no quality of life, I was not sure if I could do the job in Portland, because I guess I must have sensed something weird was going on with Robert.

When I came back to Phoenix to get ready for moving, I went to the spa at Camelback Inn with a friend. We were having lunch, and she detected my ambivalence about moving to Portland. I went home that day and went to bed, curling up in fetal position. Jon called on the phone, and I told him I was sick. And he said he hoped I was feeling better. And I said, "No I am really sick, like mentally ill. I'm not sleeping at night, and I am very worried about moving to Oregon." He came right over; he lived close by. He gave me some sleeping pills to help me sleep and crawled into bed with me and comforted me.

And then it came to me. I couldn't go. I decided that I just couldn't go. I was too vulnerable and could lose the job and with a bigger house payment, where would I be? Portland was a smaller community, and fewer programming jobs there.

Once I made the decision, I felt fine. But I had a lot of difficult work to do. I had to call PGE and tell them I wasn't taking the job. I had to call the realtor in Portland and tell her I wouldn't be buying the house; I lost my $2000 deposit, but that was a small thing. Then I called the realtor in Phoenix. I had a clause in my contract that said if I didn't have a job the contract was void. The buyer wanted to sue. I got a lawyer, but nothing happened.

The moving company was coming to pack up my house, and I canceled that. And I was having a going away party with about thirty people invited. Should I cancel? No. I decided to have the party anyway. And when everyone was gathered on the patio drinking beer and wine, I said, "Listen up everyone. I have an important announcement to make. My going away party has turned into a coming home party. I am not moving to Portland." And everyone cheered.

As it turned out that was a wise move, because my life was about to become even more complicated.

Chapter Eighteen

Mother is gone. But she had not been with us for a couple of years. After she had the stroke, she didn't even recognize me when I went to visit her. She was suffering. Unable to east, she had to be tube fed and was bedridden and on a diaper, and she wouldn't be getting any better. I felt that it was a blessing when she passed away. We were never very close, and I am sorry about that. We had much in common. She loved to read, and I think she would have been good at writing. She loved to travel, although she had a fear of flying, so she was conflicted when taking any trips that involved being on aircraft. She and Roy did have a wonderful trip to Europe, and she was able to visit her beloved Paris and the Loire Valley in France. They spent two months traveling the continent to Switzerland and then Oslo, visiting some of Roy's relatives there. As I was sorting through the mementos, I found her diary of the trip and brochures and souvenirs. It was the trip of her life, and I am so glad she had that.

She loved nature, especially birds. There were little ceramic bird figurines everywhere in her house, and I brought those back with me. She encouraged me to cook, which I still enjoy doing, and I remember how we cooked together before a holiday meal. I brought back some of her cookbooks and recipes. I think she had a sweet personality and people liked her. But Mother had a long and difficult life, especially with having to contend with Robert, who was always a problem for her even though she many times saw me as more of the problem in her life. That was true when I was in my teen years, but fortunately as an adult, I had faced life squarely and resolved my issues. Robert never did.

I was back in Phoenix and out of work again after quitting the job in Portland, where I had worked for one week. Fortunately my former employer, Charles Schwab, paid me for a couple of months even though I had quit to go to Portland. I think it was benefits for death in the family. Charles Schwab is an employee-friendly company, based in California.

Fortunately computer jobs were plentiful in Phoenix at the time, and in the past few years I had gained valuable job skills that were in demand. So I interviewed with several companies and finally took a job with a consulting firm in downtown Phoenix that was developing applications for a large firm in town. It was good work, the people were nice and the commute was an easy one from my house. I was working on an application to capture stock market quotes as they came off the wire. The company sent me to Chicago to get more information on how this data was sent. The company wanted me to come back the same day, but there was a storm, it was summer and our flight couldn't get into O'Hare on time. We had to spend the night and I was taken out for an amazing steak dinner. The next day I visited the Chicago Board of Trade and was down on the floor during trading hours. It was so exciting watching mostly men running around with tickets, recording prices as they came across. They did this with paper and pen, not electronically which surprised me. I am sure that has changed now.

BATTLE OF THE WILLS

After Mother died, I was waiting for Robert, whom Mother had designated as executor of her trust, to start transferring my half of the estate. I had received two annuities but there was some cash, and he would have to pay me half of the value of the house in Redlands. But it wasn't happening. So I hired a trust attorney to look into it. And then three months into the year, I was served with the law suit. For three long years, I fought a good fight, eventually prevailing and getting my half of the estate. Needless to say, I had little or no contact with him during this time, and then cut all relations with him when the suit was resolved. I thought of him often, though and wished I could help him, but I knew that was not to be. He had his new boyfriend, and he had other friends as well, so he wasn't alone.

Alan was now in Northern California working for Lucas Films. I would go and visit a couple of times a year, and he came to Phoenix at Christmas, sometimes bringing a girlfriend. I felt that he was on his way to a good life, and I didn't have to worry about him any longer. But then Lucas began divesting itself of all union employees, which meant that his job would be gone since he was with the union. He made the transition, freelancing and working on his own and today he is doing very well. He knows many people in the industry and that certainly helps him.

Alan was living in a basement apartment in Fairfax, California, a funky small town turned upscale. The man who owned the house where he was living told him that he was going to renovate his house and the apartment would no longer be available. I was encouraging Alan to buy a home. All of our family were home owners. Owning a home was better than renting; you gain equity in a house and have more control over payments. However house prices in the Bay Area, as everyone knows, are literally through the roof. Alan looked and found his little home in Petaluma and wanted to buy it, but he would need some additional cash down to be able to close the deal. I was working and had more than enough to live on, and I had some money from my inheritance, and I thought helping Alan would be the right thing to do.

He bought the house, and when he first moved there, he said he didn't like Petaluma. Of course, maybe it wasn't as picturesque as Fairfax, but I went to visit and I thought Petaluma was a cute little town. And now I think he loves living there.

The next few years for me were filled with hard work and trying to save for my retirement. I was in my 60's now and that day was coming fast. I quit the job with the consulting firm and was hired to program client server apps for the Arizona Republic in the circulation area; i.e. getting the paper out. The first week I was there, we were given a midnight tour of the printing presses in North Phoenix and then taken to see the distribution centers where they handed out the newspapers to the delivery people. It was pretty interesting although a long night. I think I got home about 6 a.m. that morning, but I didn't have to be at work that day.

I also remember—I think it was my first week—management called all of the department into a meeting and told us that we were all expected to work 50 hours a week, not just the 40 hours that were normally required of an employee. Some companies were known as what we called sweat shops and I thought at the time, this is one of those. There are labor laws, but because Arizona is a right-to-work state, those laws were not enforced and there were few unions supporting the workers. I was a salaried worker as well and that was a factor. As we walked out of the meeting, I heard several people grumbling that they were getting their resume ready; they would be looking elsewhere for a job. And I don't blame them. I just blew it off, thinking I'll do what I think is best and if they fire me, oh well. There was always another job. My how things have changed since the Bush depression in 2008 with fewer jobs available, and plummeting salaries and wages. Good for management, bad for the workers.

In addition, what I didn't know when I was hired was that the programmers on the circulation team had to be on call on a rotation basis. After a couple of weeks on the job, they handed me a pager and told me that I was "it" for the weekend. I had never had a job before where I had to be on call. My job at Intel was extremely difficult as I was handed two applications to work on the day I walked in the door. I was the analyst and the programmer, and I was expected to take classes in addition, which was about 60 hours a week with a long commute to Chandler from my house. But now, once a month I would have to be available all weekend to answer calls and fix the data, making sure the paper got out on time. And this was main frame, which I didn't know. We had desk top applications capturing the data and storing it on a database, and then the data was dumped onto the main frame. Many companies operated this way, especially when there were large amounts of data to be processed. So there were about 100 processes running all night long, and they failed sometimes, usually due to problems with the data itself. Maybe someone would put quotes around a name when they were entering it, and there wasn't any error coding to handle that. It was my job to find the error and fix it. Sometimes I would get a call at 2 a.m., and I would be up the rest of the night finding and fixing it. If it was a Sunday night, I would have to be at work as usual. I recall saying to them that it would be advantageous to do some error coding to prevent the failures—duh. They did take my advice, so as time went on there were fewer failures.

Other than that, it was a fun job. People were nice, I made some good friends there. One of the perks was that every month they had a book sale offering books that had been sent to the newspaper for review. I loved that and often went home with an armload of wonderful books, some that weren't even in the bookstores yet.

I remember I was working at the newspaper when 9/11 happened. I watched the first airplane hit the tower on TV as I was getting ready for work. I went into the office that morning and a special meeting was called to tell everyone that we would have to have someone covering 24/7. They set up shifts, and I took the first shift, 5p.m. to midnight. I went back home and rested to prepare for the nighttime shift and then went back to work at 5. It was a slow night, nothing happened, and I got a lot of work done. But when I was getting ready to go home, because it was so late and the parking garage was a couple of buildings over from our office building, I asked the guard to escort me to my car, and he was obliging to do that. When we walked out of the building, there was an eerie silence before two fighter jets flew over the downtown area.

What did this all mean? Would we be going to war? On the news I heard Bush a couple of days after the disaster asking Cheney if we could now attack Iraq. And then the buildup to war began. Within several weeks they sent troops to Afghanistan as they thought Bin Laden was responsible for the attack, and he was allegedly training terrorists there. But it was Saudis who flew the airplanes. I was confused because all flights in and out of the country were canceled. But then, a dozen or so of bin Laden's family who had been visiting Bush, were flown out of the country a day or so after the event.

The march to war intensified using 9/11 as the excuse. After studying the collapse of the buildings, I and some others came to realize it wasn't the planes that had brought down the towers but some explosives that had been placed at an earlier time in the basement. They were trying to make us believe that the fuel from the airplanes melted the steel and collapsed the buildings. But if you watch the video, that fuel burned upward very quickly and never reached the steel at the bottom. Building seven collapsed and it wasn't even hit. But people were in a daze and they believed everything they were told by the Bush administration. And there was a lot of patriotism in the country.

I and some others suspected that this was an inside job, but the truth would never come out. Even with the sham investigation later run by the Bush/Cheney administration.

I had started to write my memoir, but decided to write a novel instead about a president taking his country to war under false pretenses. I wrapped the story around his wife, the first lady divorcing him while he was running for re-election. I tried to find an agent and then a publisher, but that is always difficult if you aren't an established author, so I decided to self-publish. I created a publishing company, Verde Press and set up an s-corp. I then found an editor who also designed the interior of the book, and found a local graphics company to create the cover according to my design. I searched for and found a printing company in North Carolina. Several weeks later a truck rolled up to my house and deposited several cartons with 2,000 books in my driveway. Being that I live in a very small house with minimal storage space, I was stashing book cartons everywhere, behind chairs, under tables.

I told a few people at work about my book being published and several people purchased it. Some of these people were in agreement with me; the war was unnecessary, a waste of lives and money, and a mistake. But there were others who wouldn't even talk to me after reading it. Of course now we know, too late, that this war was one of the biggest blunders our country has ever made.

I marketed the book to local book stores, Barnes and Noble and Borders, which is no longer in business. They were very good to me and brought me into the stores to do book signings. I then traveled to Tucson and Flagstaff and had signing events in the book stores in those cities as well.

I then decided to write a sequel to *The President's Wife*, *Madam POTUS*. The story continues where i after being exiled with her son in Europe, Carol, the first lady, comes back to the United States and runs for the senate. After serving a term, she runs and wind the election to be our first woman president. Unfortunately, the only one we have at this writing.

I traveled to Paris to do research for the book as some of the story takes place in France. This was my first trip to Europe, and I loved it. I traveled with a friend, Eileen Wallace, who was an artist. We flew to London spending a day there, and then boarded the Euro Train that took us through the Chunnel. Very fun. We disembarked at Gare du Nord in Paris. I had mapped out where our hotel was, thinking we could walk from the train station. We got lost, ending up way south near the Louvre and ended up taking a cab anyway. Contrary to what people say, Parisians were very friendly and helpful, and we didn't speak but a few words of French. We both enjoyed being in Paris, visiting the museums, the Eiffel Tower, eating at sidewalk cafes. We took the train to Palace of Versailles, which is an amazing place. I mention that Eileen was an artist working in water color. I have one of her beautiful paintings hanging in my living room. Sadly a couple of years later after our trip together, she contracted lymphoma and passed away, and I think she was only in her fifties.

I published *Madam POTUS* with iUniverse, a vanity publishing company. It was an exercise in futility. I lost control of my work, and we fought about almost everything. I have since pulled *Madam POTUS* away from them and republished under my own company, Verde Press.

In 2005 I retired from the newspaper, I had been there for five years and received a small pension. I was sixty-five now and it was time to hang up my programmer's hat. However I received an offer from a small software development company located in East Mesa. They made me an offer I couldn't refuse. The company provided a windows application for large insurance companies. I said I would work for a year or two at the most. I could increase my retirement fund and add more to my Social Security. Well, I ended up working there for three years. In 2008, the Bush depression hit and that fall my boss called me in and said that it wasn't because of my work being substandard, but they were laying off half the people in the company, about ten. I remember that day so well. I went back to my desk and cleaned out my things. I didn't know whether to laugh or cry as I was driving home. I had lost the big salary, but now I could write full time.

What I didn't know then was that there was more trouble ahead. In fact, the fight of my life.

Chapter Nineteen

When I arrived home that day after being laid off, I sat down at my kitchen table to do a budget, and I thought to myself, it's time for heaven's sake. I am sixty eight years old. I have considerable savings built up. I can start collecting Social Security, and I will have Medicare for my health needs. What do I need a job for at this point in my life? Originally I had, however, thought I would work until I was seventy, but it looked like that wouldn't happen. I would look at the job market and see if it was possible to get another job, but I was doubtful I would find one with the country sinking into a depression.

My next task was to go to DES, Department of Economic Security, and put in a claim for unemployment insurance. The company didn't give me any severance, which was pretty tacky, but if I could collect unemployment for a couple of months, that would tide me over until I could get my finances in order. That is if the company approved it, and I thought they would. I wasn't fired for cause, which can prevent DES from paying benefits.

I had savings. I was debt free; no car payments, no credit card payments or department store debt. The only real debt that I had was the remaining mortgage on my house, which by that time, at

27 years on a 30 year mortgage, was minimal. So that was my next task, pay off the house and I would have more to live on.

The next day I went to the Social Security office in Scottsdale and filed a claim to start my payments and sign up for Medicare. They looked at my record and asked if I wanted to collect under my first husband's account. If a woman is married to someone for more than ten years you can do that and that's good for women who have not been able to make enough on their own. But I had worked for twelve years in the computer industry and hopefully accrued enough benefits for me to collect on my own account, so I said no.

I did contact some employment agencies to see if there was anything available for me. What I found was that there were jobs out there but nothing in Phoenix. Jobs in Minneapolis, Rochester Minnesota, New York City, Washington DC, Mobile Alabama — Manhattan which could have been fun. I had a phone interview with the company from Mobile, and I completely blew it as I was so tired from not sleeping the few days before. I've always hated phone interviews; there is no eye contact and no way of knowing what the interviewers are thinking. No loss, I would not have wanted to move to Mobile anyway. So after a few weeks, I gave up, although I kept getting emails looking for Powerbuilder programmers, which was the area that I had expertise in.

After a time I settled in to being "retired". But no, that wasn't the original plan. I would be writing full time instead of trying to find time on the weekends in between taking care of a house and two dogs and all that involves. In the next few months I wrote what I call my recession novel: a story of rescue, *She Sleeps with Dogs*. Jasmine, a middle-aged woman loses her job and then has to put down her best friend dog of many years. She volunteers for the Humane Society and brings home a dog to foster and eventually adopts him and names him Chance. In this story, Chance has a voice and sometimes tells his side of what is happening. Her daughter, Celeste, calls from Los Angeles, and she has lost her job as well, has no place to live and asks her mother if she can come and live with her. Jasmine of course says yes. How could she refuse her only daughter? But when Celeste brings her boyfriend, Jasmine has to say no to him staying there. Jasmine takes in another dog that was abandoned at the dog park and that dog is pregnant. Then Celeste becomes pregnant, and her boyfriend has left the country. It's a slice of life book that people have told me is a joy to read.

When I look back at those days after losing my job, I don't know where they went. They were happy days. I spent time with friends; I now had time to go to lunch and enjoy it. I was running a couple of days a week, climbing Piestewa Peak every Friday. I gardened and did some redecorating of my house, painting my bedroom a soothing ocean green, buying Victorian lace valences to put over the new cellular shades that I had bought. I had also bought a new patio set, a settee, two chairs and coffee table, and I was spending more time on the patio reading, listening and watching the birds.

I cooked, making prickly pear jelly and syrup from the fruit I collected from plants in the neighborhood. It was so good, and I wish I had time to do that again.

The years went by, and then for my 70th birthday, my son invited me to have a weekend in Yosemite National Park the weekend of May 27th of that year. I was delighted. A whole weekend in a beautiful place hiking and exploring with the person I loved most, my wonderful son.

He planned everything. I flew to California the day before, he met me at the Oakland Airport, and we drove to Yosemite from there. We stayed in the Curry Village tent cabins, sleeping on cots. It was spring, still quite cool and he had brought a small space heater to keep us warm. He gave me a little bag of camping items, soap and some other essentials. He also gave me a pair of trekking poles, which I didn't have. Those poles over the years have been a help navigating trails in some faraway places.

    The day of my birthday, we hiked up the trail to Vernal Falls, and it was exquisitely beautiful. I remember that day on the trail telling everyone we met that it was my birthday and I was 70 years old. I was healthy and strong enough to hike up this rather steep trail. That night as I was getting ready for dinner, taking a shower in the communal shower building for women, I was soaping my body and for some reason I felt my right breast and noticed a lump. I immediately thought I had better have that checked when I get home. I hadn't had a mammogram in a couple of years.

    Alan took me for dinner that evening in the dining room of the historic Ahwahnee Hotel in the park. We had a view of the mountains from the window by our table, and the pianist played vintage music from the 50's and 60's. It was a most wonderful birthday.

After I came home from my birthday celebration in California, I got caught up in the daily activities and didn't go to the doctor as I had said I would. The summer went by very quickly even though it was very hot; but that is Arizona.

    Then in September, I was getting dressed to go hiking and I felt movement in my right breast. That was the one that I had felt the lump in when I was showering at Yosemite. I guess I had better go to the doctor and have it checked out immediately. Something was very wrong.

    I called the doctor and they had me come right in. This is a doctor that I have been going to for 20 years or more. After he examined me, he looked me straight in the eye and said, "Do you want to die Elaine?"

    "No," I said. "I have too much to live for. I want to live."

BATTLE OF THE WILLS

He made an appointment with an imaging doctor so we could better see what we were dealing with. And, yes there was a lump. They would take some tissue and do a biopsy to determine whether it was cancerous or not. But I knew it probably was cancer. I was devastated. I shouldn't be having this; there is no history of breast cancer in my family. Grandma died of colon cancer, not breast cancer. But yes, it was true. And it was likely caused by my taking female hormones during menopause.

I was shaken and in a daze. I called Alan and told him, and he said he would come to Arizona when and if I needed him. He was right there for me.

I was sent to a breast surgeon. He was an okay doctor, but there was something about him; I didn't like the way he talked to me. A friend recommended a female breast surgeon so I went to see her in North Scottsdale, a long drive for me, but I felt more comfortable with a female doctor.

After they determined that it was cancerous, I went to see an oncologist, and it sounded like he thought I shouldn't have the aggressive treatment of chemo therapy, that I wouldn't do well with it. He recommended treating the cancer with some drugs that I would take by mouth. That didn't sound right to me. This was a large tumor. And if it metastasized, I would likely die. I talked with my surgeon and she sent me to another oncologist—female this time—who said that we should get started right away; there was no time to lose. I was confused, getting mixed messages, but then I agreed, I wanted this cancer to be gone and the sooner the better. I thought I would be strong enough to withstand chemo treatment. The plan was to shrink the 8 CM tumor with chemo and then remove the breast.

I was sad; I had nice breasts that had filled out for the first time in my life; my breasts had always been little. And now I was going to lose one. But I knew it was better to lose a breast than to lose my life—no question.

As soon as I had been diagnosed, I started researching breast cancer, the cures, and ways that I could assist the doctors in fighting this disease that had invaded my body. If I was going to go, I wasn't going quietly. I would fight this with everything that I had. I looked at alternative natural cures and even went to a naturopathic doctor, whom I soon realized was a quack. I then decided that an aggressive approach would be best along with natural methods; modifying my diet, taking supplements with the approval of my doctor and exercise. We would become partners in fighting my cancer.

I had my first chemo treatment the week before Thanksgiving. A couple of weeks before that, I had cut my long hair as I knew I would be losing it soon. I purchased a wig that looked much like my natural hair. The week before I was to have treatment, I had a surgically inserted port on the left side just above my breast that would allow the doctor to insert a syringe to administer the chemicals that went straight into my blood stream eliminating the need to put a syringe in my vein every time I had chemo.

The day I was scheduled for treatment, I drove myself to the oncologists' office and sat in the waiting room feeling very apprehensive. I had heard horror stories about what it was like to have chemo therapy. The chemo I would get the first two months was said to be very strong. I was prepared to be very sick with nausea and vomiting, loss of appetite and who knows what else.

The doctor checked my vitals, and then I was taken to the chemo room with several lazy boy chairs for patients to sit in. There was one other patient in the room receiving chemo, and she was surrounded by her family who were comforting her. I was alone, but I didn't mind. I could handle this; I would get through this terrible time in my life.

After I sat in the chair, the nurse inserted the syringe into my

BATTLE OF THE WILLS

port and started the drip of the liquid poison into my body. And that's precisely what it is. I remember the tingling feeling in my whole body as the chemo entered my blood stream and began to circulate throughout my body.

An hour later I was released and sent home. Surprisingly I felt well enough to drive and the doctor told me I would be able to during my treatments that I would receive every other week. I had been given prescriptions for nausea and I think a tranquilizer, and I took them as the doctor had ordered. The next day I had to return to the doctor for a Neulasta shot, an antidote to boost my immune system and minimize the bad effects of the chemo on my body. I soon found out that this shot, manufactured by one of the big pharmaceutical producers, cost $8,000 per shot. I would be having four of them; do the math, $32,000 just for that one shot every other week. My insurance covered most of this cost, but I thought that it was outrageous to charge that much money for this shot, and I in fact called the pharmaceutical company to tell them so.

That week after the first treatment, I felt lousy, like I had a bad case of the flu. I slept a lot and I had no appetite, but I wasn't vomiting thank goodness. That next week, I started to feel better. That would be the routine; one week of being sick and then a week of recovery, and then back to being sick again. I learned to plan my activities around this regimen.

Thanksgiving was here and Alan was coming to see me. I picked him up at the airport and brought him home. As much as I loved cooking for him and his girlfriend's when they came to visit, I wasn't up for it this holiday, and so we purchased some food and had a small celebration at home. I had to tell everyone not to touch my hair; it was falling out and I wanted to keep it as long as I could.

November, December, the two months of strong chemo were almost over. I had started walking every day and especially on the days I had treatment, and I felt much better. Christmas, Alan came again and we had a small celebration. My good friend, Ralph, took some photos of Alan and me together.

Chapter Twenty

It was the New Year. I had completed the first two months of the rigorous chemo treatment, and the tumor was shrinking. That meant our strategy was working. I had changed doctors, back to the first oncologist I had seen in the fall. The other doctor was loading me up on other drugs along with the chemo, and I ended up in the emergency ward one morning. I had a new breast surgeon as well, one the present oncologist recommended, a woman who was highly thought of in the valley. It had taken a long time, but I felt I had the team that would do the best for me.

It was on to the second phase of my treatment; Taxol was given to me once a week. The doctor explained that this drug was designed to clean up any cancer that might have escaped into other areas of my body. The caveat was that my vitals had to be in good order every week in order to take this, and he said I might have to skip a week every so often. But that was not my plan. I would be healthy enough every week; I wanted to get through this phase as quickly as possible. I was walking every day and started jogging again on Sunday. I began climbing Piestuwa on Friday as I had done before I started chemo; that first time I went as far as I could until I was back to what I had always done.

I had limited my diet as well. No sugar. I used honey if I wanted a sweetener. No coffee or alcohol. Bummer. I had a cleansing drink that I took a couple of times a week, and I was juicing and eating lots of green veggies and black bean soup.

The first couple of weeks of Taxol were going well, and I didn't feel nearly as sick as I had on the other chemo. But before the nurse gave the chemo, she had to give me Benadryl, and it knocked me out so much that I asked if she could cut the dose in half, which she did. So when I was having Taxol, I would basically go to sleep. Then I had to have someone drive me to and from the doctor every week. What was so wonderful was I really found out who my friends were and that I had more than I thought. People were fighting over taking me to chemo.

And I had met another lady before Christmas in the chemo room. She was zany, wearing a red wig, laughing and cracking jokes, and I started talking with her. She was so full of joy. I found out that she had lung cancer, and it had metastasized and was in many areas of her body. I knew what that meant, and so did she. But she was making the best of a bad situation. They were trying to eradicate it, although it wasn't looking good. But she had this attitude; she was always smiling and laughing and happy. I loved her.

We became friends, and she would come and sit with me sometimes when I was getting the Taxol, and I appreciated it.

I went every week for my Taxol treatment. They tested my blood every time, and I passed with flying colors and the technician said whatever I was doing was working. I never missed one treatment. I was determined to beat this cancer thing and get on with my life. I had too much living to do.

At the end of the three months of Taxol, I was feeling pretty well, except I was losing some toenails, my fingernails had ridges and I had tingling in my fingers and toes. My sinuses were a wreck as well, but other than that....

BATTLE OF THE WILLS

Now for the next phase. The doctor made an appointment for a full body MRI scan to see if any of the cancer had spread. If it had, I would be in stage 4, I would not have the surgery and it would be a matter of time before I would die. But if the cancer had not spread, we would move forward with the surgery.

I went for the full body scan. Then the next week I went to get the results. My life was hanging in the balance. Either it would be thumbs up you live, or you're going to die. The facility was located in Scottsdale across from Fashion Square, a huge shopping mecca in Scottsdale, which I normally don't patronize. I parked my car, I walked into the office and asked for my results. The woman at the front desk searched for my envelope and then she handed it to me and said good luck. I wondered what she meant by that. I walked out to my car to read the results in private. Gingerly opening the envelope, I looked inside and then pulled out the report. It said that my body, other than my breast, was clear of any cancer. I WAS CLEAR. I cried. For the first time, I cried. And then I went shopping.

I have this friend. I've known him for over ten years now. I met him while I was working at one of the companies as a programmer. His name is Ralph. I have to say he is my very best friend in the whole world. I have said very little about him, but I have to talk about him now, because during my cancer he was there for me at every turn. He took me to emergency that early morning when I was so sick. He took me to chemo. He would come to my house and help me build my cancer blog and another web site as well.

Over the years Ralph has been with me on Christmas, New Year's, other holidays, my birthday and he often comes over on weekends for dinner. I have to say that I love this man, as a friend. We once talked of dating and becoming more than friends, but I couldn't see it. For one thing, he is seventeen years younger than me. But we continue our friendship, and I am grateful to have him.

My dogs love him as well, and he comes and lives with them when I travel, for which I pay him.

The doctors moved up my surgery by two weeks, and April 13th I went into the surgical center in Scottsdale. My surgeon had asked me when I first met with her if I wanted to remove both breasts. I know some people do that, with the thought that they would not be vulnerable for cancer in the healthy breast. But I wanted to keep my one healthy breast and take my chances. Losing both breasts would have been much more traumatic, especially when I didn't have to.

Alan had come to be with me, and he drove me to the surgical center that early morning and waited there until I was out of recovery. The surgery went well, the only complication was that I was sick from the anesthesia and continued to vomit for a couple of hours after I was awake.

My chest was bound with gauze and tape and I felt my right side and it was flat; my breast was gone. The surgeon removed all of my lymph nodes on the right side as well and told me later that 7 of the 9 lymph nodes were cancerous; the cancer was getting ready to spread. Lucky? Blessed? Whatever you want to call it, I had escaped an early death.

The nurses were wonderful at the surgical center. They brought me whatever I needed, all hours of the day and night that I was there. The first afternoon after surgery, I was encouraged to get up and walk, and Alan was there to help and guide me on my unsteady legs. But by the next morning, I was feeling much stronger, no longer sick to my stomach, eating and doing all of the things I was supposed to be doing, and the doctor said I could go home.

The doctor sent me home with pain medication, but amazingly I had very little pain, and so I didn't take any of it, instead taking an Advil a couple of times.

The next morning, I was feeling restless and so I said to Alan

BATTLE OF THE WILLS

that we should go to South Mountain, a mountainous city park in South Phoenix, and go hiking. And we did. I could only hike a short distance, but it was wonderful being out in the warm fresh air. On the way back, we stopped at the main library in Phoenix on Central Avenue.

Then it was time for Alan to go home, and I was on my own. That next week I went to the doctor to have my bandages removed. I had a drain, a small plastic bottle attached with a tube under my skin to remove the excess liquid that was coming from the surgical area. When the doctor removed the bandages, I looked at the right side of my chest where my breast used to be and saw the stitches where they had cut away the breast. But I was alive, I said to myself. And I had things to do and places to go.

But I still had to have radiation to complete my treatment. Several weeks later, I don't recall how long, I went for my first radiation therapy. Again I didn't know what to expect. The technician carefully measured the area that would be radiated and marked it with tattoos, little blue dots on my skin, which was very painful; actually more painful than anything I had to this point. Then I went back the next day, and they started the treatment. The huge radiation machine is in a special room, and the technician positions the machine in the area to be treated and the radiation kills off any cancer cells that might remain. Of course it kills some healthy cells as well, but they try to keep that to a minimum. For 37 days, every day, except weekends, I went to have this treatment.

Compared to what I had already endured, this was the easy part. I wasn't sick afterward. In fact, I felt energized, had lost weight; and had my little teenage figure back. The mistake I made was buying some clothes that fit this little figure; clothes that now sit in my closet—I am unable to get into them now.

And so I began my second life; AC, After Cancer. BC, before

cancer, I had a wish list of things I wanted to do and places I wanted to visit and now it was time. That fall, I was invited to attend a friends' birthday party in Puerto Vallarta. Judy and I had worked together at Intel in Chandler, and she had since moved to Portland, Oregon, still with Intel. She had rented a mansion and invited about a dozen of her best friends and family. Should I go? Was I strong enough? I decided to chance it. And I had a wonderful time. I loved the city, and spent time just wandering the streets, watching the people. The beach was so peaceful and beautiful. I also made another friend there, Elisabeth, who was also from Portland. We hopped on a peso bus one morning and headed up the coast to the little fishing village of Sayulita and hung out on the beach there. She spoke fluent Spanish which was a help. We had dinner one night on the beach and ate huge shrimp as the moon came up over the mountains to the east—mesmerizing.

Another day, we boarded a boat, sailing out into the Bay of Banderas to an area down the coast where we snorkeled. I remember sitting on the back of the sail boat next to the captain. He looked at me, asked how I felt and said I looked a little green. And sure enough minutes later I was throwing up over the side of the boat. Never in my life had I ever had motion sickness. I was a flight attendant and had been on bumpy rides on aircraft with others getting sick all around me and I never did. I was on a large 40 foot sail boat that went to Catalina Island; I was never sick. Why now?

I went ahead and snorkeled with a little help from my friends, and then lay on the beach of the small fishing village where we stopped to have lunch. Someone gave me a Dramamine for the ride back, and I felt better.

But overall, I had a great time. After that trip, I felt that I could travel and see some of the places around the world that I had been thinking about for so long.

Chapter Twenty-One

A month after I finished radiation, I threw out the special diet and went back to my old habits. Coffee never tasted better. I was eating cookies and chocolate and ice cream and loving it. A beer or wine with dinner was sublime. I was among the living again. I was also back to my usual exercise routine: jogging five miles on Sunday, walking most days and climbing the mountain on Friday. Just breathing in the fresh air as I was jogging made me feel alive and realize how fortunate I was to be outside, healthy again and ready to live my life to the fullest.

Reflecting back, I have to be thankful that I had a wonderful team of doctors who did the right thing for me with my oversight. One must realize that treating a serious illness, or any illness for that matter, is always a doctor patient partnership. I do think my change in lifestyle and continuing my exercise routine helped me come through this dreadful disease. The one question that I still wonder is, what was the true cause? And why isn't the medical community focusing on that aspect of cancer? One answer might be, cancer is a huge industry and until we get the money out of health care in this country, it will continue to be that way. If a cure is found, then prevention is next, and if cancer can be prevented, the oncologists, radiologists, hospitals, pharma will not make money. It's that simple.

I am thankful too for all the support from my friends and family and my son who was right there whenever I needed him.

By the following year I was getting back to normal, my energy level was up and I was feeling really good and ready for the next phase of my life; After Cancer. It was time to hit the road. Or explicitly, get on an airplane and travel. The only question was, would I travel alone, or with group or find a friend to travel with? My first trip that year took me to Italy where I attended a writing workshop in a 12th century hilltop town with a rustic hotel. I flew into Rome and spent my first day there visiting the Vatican Art museum, and then I toured the Coliseum which was about a block away from my hotel. Rome is a city where you can walk most everywhere. The next day, I met my group and we boarded a bus that took us to Santo Stefano di Sessanio, the hilltop village in the mountains of Abruzzo, about 90 miles east of Rome. It was so lovely, and I celebrated my birthday the first night I was there.

I had a beautiful room on the corner of the medieval hotel with a fireplace and windows that overlooked the valley all around. When I opened the door to my room, there were a dozen red roses from Ralph. I was blown away. What a sweet thing for him to do. At dinner that night in the restaurant in the town, they brought me a birthday cake. I had so much wine that night that I was a little under the weather the next day. But I recovered.

There were eight of us in the group. We started every morning in this little café having a frittata and wonderful breads with juice and coffee, and then we spent the rest of the morning writing and critiquing. In the afternoon, we enjoyed cultural immersion events in the area. One day we went to see another hilltop town, and another day we visited a sheep farm where they made cheese products, and another we saw a demonstration in the village of making pasta. I loved it.

Six days later we were back in Rome and I was taking off on my own, catching the train to Florence where I would visit museums and cathedrals and hang out in the plaza of the Duomo. I stayed in a convent run by French nuns who spoke very little English. When I arrived the first evening, I went to my very austere room, only 40 euros a night. It had a small twin bed, a washbowl and a small desk and the bathroom was down the hall. But then I opened the shutters and before me was a beautiful garden full of flowers, and I could hear the nuns singing vespers.

Every day I walked all over the city. I fell in love with David, the magnificent Renaissance statue by Michelangelo. I visited the Ufizzi gallery and saw magnificent Italian Renaissance paintings. I visited the Museo Galileo where I saw science exhibits and instruments of the 13th century. Every afternoon I went to the piazza Duomo to have Gelato. But a funny thing happened to me in Florence. As I was checking out to leave, the nun said to me in broken English, "You were supposed to leave yesterday." And I looked at the calendar and, sure enough, I had stayed an extra day longer. I had been so wrapped up in the city that I forgot what day it was. Problem was, I was due to catch a flight out of Rome later that afternoon. Too funny. No matter. I caught the first train out of Florence and arrived in Rome late that morning. I had a few hours before I had to be at the airport, so I left my luggage at the hotel where I was supposed to stay the night before; they were very understanding about my not showing up. I walked to the Trevi Fountain and to the Pantheon and came back to the hotel to catch my taxi to the airport, about a twenty mile ride. All together it was a wonderful trip and I liked the idea of being with the group and then going off on my own. I wrote an article about Italy, and it was published in an on line magazine.

So with my first foray into traveling underway, where should I go next? Something exotic, I thought. How about Africa?

For this type of trip I was thinking I should travel with a group. I knew Sierra Club had international trips so I went online to see what they had going to Africa. I saw a trip that sounded fascinating, a ten day safari in the bush of Botswana. I signed up immediately.

That next February, I flew to Johannesburg South Africa, stopping briefly in Dakar Senegal to board a new crew for the 17 hour flight. Some have asked me how I tolerate the long international flights, and I have to say that I love them. For me it's thoroughly enjoyable. The airlines wine and dine you on these flights; the food is not bad and they serve complimentary wine and after dinner drinks. It's a party. I meet people from all over the world, and sometimes I go back to the galley and hang out with the flight attendants. And then I go back to my seat and take a nap. By that time, we are usually at our destination. But I was a flight attendant in another life.

I spent a day in Joberg and then we flew to Maun Botswana where our guides met us to take us back into the bush. We piled into the Land Rovers and headed toward the bush, and it took us all of an afternoon and part of the evening to get there, starting on a paved road, which soon became a rough gravel road, and morphed into a bush trail. We were tired and dusty, but when we were finally close to our camp, a cheetah crossed the trail, and it was all worth it. When we rounded the corner, a huge campfire appeared along with a table with lanterns; it was like something out of the movies. Every day we went on game drives and saw wonderful animals: elephants, leopards, lions, hippopotamus, giraffe, zebra, wart hogs, and the list goes on. The beautiful part was that the animals were in their natural habitat, doing what they always do. We saw a cheetah kill a wart hog right in front of our land rover. We saw an elephant that had been brought down by a pride of lions.

BATTLE OF THE WILLS

We moved camp every few days and eventually came into Chobe National Park, where there were so many elephants and crocodiles. Then on to Victoria Falls, where the morning we were leaving to go back home, I had a guide take me across the top of the falls, which was dry as it was fall there, and to Livingston Island, where I got into a pool at the top of the falls and looked over the edge. Breathtaking.

I came home and wrote another article which was published, and decided that I would write a novel. I remembered Satao, the beautiful bull elephant that had recently been killed for his ivory in Tsavo National Park in Kenya, Africa, and I decided that I wanted to write about the plight of elephant poaching in Africa. *Murder on Safari* is a story about a war correspondent who is sent to Kenya to report on the poaching of elephants. She says she doesn't do that type of reporting but decides to go anyway and falls in love with Africa, the elephants and a park ranger. It was published a year later.

That fall, I went to the Bavarian Alps, hiking and enjoying German beer and hospitality. Flying into Munich, I met our group, and we had a bus with a driver who took us on a tour of Bavaria beginning with Berchtesgaden, actually Hitler's hangout. Those first couple of nights I had a magnificent view of **Watzmann Mountain from my hotel balcony. I had a glass of wine every evening, watching the alpenglow on the mountain. We sailed on** Lake **Königssee** and hiked in the area. We took a bus to the Eagles Nest, Hitler's tea house retreat on the summit of the Kehlstein. Then we visited Salzburg and had a tour of The Sound of Music sites, attended a Mozart concert that evening, and the next day I toured Mozart's home. I think the highlight of this trip was the hike we did out of Garmisch, walking through the pastoral Bavarain countryside with cows and horses and other domestic animals. It was raining. We had our sack lunch under a tree and then came to a hut that was like a pub where people gathered, ate and drank beer. When we walked inside, it was warm and friendly with a fire in the fireplace. People were seated at rustic wooden tables, eating and drinking, their dogs relaxing under the tables. Our guide played the accordion, German music and some other songs, and we sang along. It gave me goose bumps.

There was so much more; an exciting gorge with water rushing through. I went to the top of Germany on a tram, and viewed the vista overlooking the Alps for miles around. When we ended our trip in Munich, I was sad to be going home.

Four years and counting. The experts say that when a cancer survivor reaches the five year mark, you are home free; the chances of the cancer coming back are greatly minimized. I had my mammograms done every year now on my remaining breast, and I was clear. I wasn't worried. And now I started thinking about reconstruction. I had a prosthesis that made me look normal when I wore a special bra, but they were heavy, silicone lumps that shifted around when I moved. I couldn't go braless without seeing that empty left side. I think my posture was bad as well because there were times when I caught myself slumping. I just felt lopsided.

First I had to decide what type of breast replacement I would have and I had two options available. One is the natural method of transferring tissue from another part of the body to the breast area and the other is inserting breast implants, usually silicone. I talked with several people, along with one friend who had the natural method, and I thought that was the way I would go. But I was limited by the availability of surgeons to perform this operation. Fortunately, my Medicare would cover the cost. Now to find a surgeon in my network to do the surgery. I finally found the doctor, made an appointment and went to see him. He would do the implant, but did not do the natural augmentation. I decided to settle for the implant method. He told me that because I had radiation, I would have to have skin tissue transferred to the breast area to support the implant. This was because the radiation made the skin in that area weak and brittle and it would not be strong enough to hold the implant. And I had two choices; either take it from the abdominal area or from my back. Immediately I said to take it from my back. I didn't want to compromise my core. This is called the latissimus flap breast reconstruction.

There would be three surgeries; the first to graft the new skin to the area and then expand it. The second to insert the permanent implant and then a follow up surgery, mainly cosmetic, to make adjustments and fashion a nipple. Yes, I was going to have a new nipple. We set a date. I had one more trip I wanted to do before I would go forward with this.

Chapter Twenty-Two

I decided my next trip would be over the top or actually at the bottom of the planet; Antarctica. Again I went to the Sierra Club web site for international trips. The last two trips were so successful. These trips were well planned and we'd had knowledgeable local guides, the best accommodations, the food was wonderful as well. Also the people were friendly and easy to get along with. But then we were all on the same wavelength, environmentalists. And I liked that. I'd had a bad experience when I went to Costa Rica with REI, New Year's 1999, turn of the century trip. Again it was a small group, but there was one woman from New York City who was constantly complaining about the weather (It was raining. We were in a rain forest for god's sake.) the food, the accommodations. She was angry because we were held up on the road to Arenal volcano for three hours due to a fatal accident. She railed on the trip leader, which I thought was terribly rude. It affected the whole group. People chose sides, and it was something like survivor. Very unpleasant. After that experience, I was hesitant to travel with a group. A couple years later, I took another trip to Vancouver Washington alone and skied at Whistler and that was fun. I always meet people when I travel solo, and I like that. I am still friends with a friend whom I met and skied with at Whistler. But there are benefits of being with the group as well. You don't get lost. If I had been with a group in Florence, I would have checked out on time. But fortunately I recovered from that mistake.

So it was off on another adventure. I booked my flights and reserved the rooms that I would need. Most of the trip, however, would be on the expedition boat. I flew to Buenos Aires, and then on to Ushuaia at the very tip of South America to begin my voyage to the seventh continent. I had problems with Argentinian Airways getting there; they actually changed my flight and didn't notify me. The flight from Houston to Buenos Aires was held up; mechanical—fuel pump on the aircraft was malfunctioning. We sat on the ground for three hours waiting. But I am accustomed to these little glitches. I did want them to have the fuel pump working properly, however as that is a strategic part in keeping the aircraft in the air.

I arrived in Ushuaia a day early, and my roommate and I looked around the town and went shopping. I picked up some wonderful souvenirs: a hat, a t-shirt, a stuffed penguin. Then it was time to board our ship and we were soon on our way into the Beagle Sound headed for the dreaded Drake, the most volatile ocean on earth where three oceans are coming together: the Atlantic, the Pacific and the Southern oceans. For three days we were tossed about, finally reaching the Antarctic Peninsula. I call this place the most beautiful on earth. It is pristine and relatively untouched by humans, likely due to the inclement weather, but it is teaming with wildlife; penguins, seals, whales and many species of birds. I won't bore you with details. You can read about it in the book that I wrote when I returned, *The Iceberg Murders*.

A month after returning from Antarctica, I had my first reconstructive surgery. Now I understand why women say it is more painful than the breast surgery. But I recovered. The next spring I went to New Zealand, traveling the length of the South Island. I was sick a good part of the time but still did some hiking and kayaking in Milford Sound, a fjord-like place surrounded by tall mountains. We stayed at a backpackers lodge with cabin-like quarters and the bathroom down the hall. At happy hour, many gathered in a lounge area for drinks and they were from all over the world. So exciting.

Back home again and another surgery, not as difficult this time and the new breast is taking form. Not exactly like my own, but good enough. And now I am living a life I never thought I would live. Every day is a joy; I look forward to waking up and writing and generally enjoying life. I am healthy and active. I have friends and spend time with them having lunch or hiking. I have two beautiful dogs, Lily a Brittainy Spaniel and Sophia a Weimaraner, who are like my children, and we go for walks and to the dog park. They make me laugh sometimes and they do sleep with me. I have a wonderful son. However I see very little of him anymore. But he is grown and gone and living his life and that is as it should be. In other words, I have an abundant life. I worked hard to get here, and planned and saved. And now I am enjoying the fruits. I am traveling the world to far away, sometimes exotic places, and I will continue to do that until I can't anymore. I meet people on my trips and make new friends all over the country and the world. It is quite amazing.

I still think about that phone call from the San Bernardino Sherriff's department. I wasn't prepared. When I severed relations with Robert, I didn't think I would ever hear from him again. But I am/was his only relative and the only one who could take care of his remains. I did think of him often and wondered how he was getting along. But I thought he had his boyfriend might have gotten married; I didn't know. And he had other friends as well. As I mentioned earlier, I thought that if he had the house free and clear and enough money in the bank, he would be okay. The problem was that, instead of investing the money, some 400,000 he had in his account in 2001, he spent it. He was broke, and he was getting ready to sell the house and spend that as well. But he got sick and wasn't well enough to carry through with that. He also almost burned the house down, which I found out from the neighbor. He was trying to start Mother's old car, and it caught fire in the garage. Fortunately someone called the fire department and they put out the fire before it did too much damage to the house.

He died a pauper, and he had few friends. His boyfriend abandoned him; he wasn't there because he cared for Robert, he was there for what he could get from him. He knew how vulnerable Robert was, and he took advantage of that. He was a thief.

There are times when I feel guilty for not staying with Robert and helping him in his later years, but I don't think that was possible. There was no helping him. He would have continued to abuse me, and I had to protect myself. I know he would have said that I was there just to get the house when actually I didn't care about getting anything. I got my half of the estate when Mother died, which was due me and that was all I cared about. Nor did I need to get anything more. I am financially sound.

Then there's my mother. I am still so sad that we never bonded because we could have been good friends. We had much in common. She loved to read and was an intellectual on some level. I saw that when I sorted through the books in the house. She loved nature, and I am thankful that my family passed that on to me. But I think Robert got in the way. She was always defending, protecting Robert, so much, that he was crippled by it; she enabled him. But then he was her enabler as well, because she was never strong enough emotionally or physically to take care of herself and be on her own. She always needed someone to help her. An example is when she went grocery shopping, she would never carry the groceries into the house herself; she had to always ask for help. What she didn't know is that if she had carried the groceries herself, that would have helped strengthen her muscles, and she might have had a healthier life. Although she lived a long time in human terms.

A sad note, when I was sorting through everything, I had brought home the desk pad that was on the little desk in my mother's bedroom. The removable blotter was old and messy looking so I took it out, turned it over and found a notice that my mother had received from the Department of Motor Vehicles dated May 17, 1995, stating her driving license was being revoked due to, and I quote, "your dementia disorder renders you incapable of operating a motor vehicle safely." She had 14 days to request a hearing. "Please surrender your Driver License, you can apply for an identification card from any DMV field office."

What a blow that must have been. Her world was getting smaller.

I see more clearly now, especially as I've been away from my family. I think when I was with them, I didn't know how to cope. No matter what I did, it was wrong. Robert was always right. When he abused me as a child, either Mother was gone or she turned the other way and he was never punished. Basically, they were an abusive family; even the dogs were abused. Mother would beat the dog with a yardstick when he misbehaved, much like she did me when I was a child, and it was no wonder every dog they had was a biter.

I sometimes ask myself why I didn't totally separate myself from them early on as an adult. I always kept in touch, called, sent greeting cards and gifts for birthdays and Christmas. As I was sorting through the things from the house, I found my cards, letters and gifts. I think it was out of duty. They were my only family, and I felt an obligation to maintain a relationship on some level. I did this at a distance, though, and I was able to have the space and hence a happiness I couldn't have being close to Mother and Robert. Mother asked me to come and live with them more than once, but I knew I couldn't have a happy life living with them. Now that I think of it, maybe that was what spurred me on to have the independence that I have. I never wanted to go back and live in that family where they would have control over me, and I did everything I could to take care of myself. And I think that was a healthy decision. One thing that I have to say, is that I was never jealous of my mother's attention to Robert. I think that was because I wanted to be away from both my mother and my brother. They would do whatever they were going to do. I couldn't stop them. I just didn't want to be involved.

I had often thought about Robert during those thirteen years of estrangement. I would sometimes pick up the phone and start to call him, but then stop myself, knowing that it would bring misery to my life. I wondered when I had calls with no one on the other line, if that was him, trying to reach out to me. Maybe he was sick or in trouble, both of which turned out to be true. But he frightened me. He had such a hatred for me and wanted to see me suffer, and I didn't want that in my life. I'd had too much of that growing up. So I never called him.

All of my life I had made a conscious effort to not be like my mother and I was always trying to get away from my mother. I know now that I can never do that; she is a part of me as I was a part of her, and I am mourning not only the loss of my mother and my brother, but the family I never had.

It's a new day. The ray of light here is that I survived. Not only did I survive, I am thriving. Alan did as well. Every day is special, and I am so happy to be alive and healthy. I have purpose in life, and I am fulfilling my dreams. I am no longer escaping. But I am running—running toward the exciting, wonderful life I have made for myself.

Explanation of cover images:

The image on the front cover is a photo of the two Hummel figurines that my mother had bought years ago and they were always perched on our mantle above the fireplace. The girl figure is named Spring Cheer and the boy, March Winds and they are a perfect metaphor for the troublesome relationship that I and my brother had. Notice the hint of jealousy as the boy eyes the serendipitous little girl.

www.ingramcontent.com/pod-product-compliance
Lightning Source LLC
Chambersburg PA
CBHW020929090426
42736CB00010B/1086